D0603547

Busy Family Recipes

Publications
International, Ltd.

Louis Weber, CEO
Publications International, Ltd.
7373 North Cicero Avenue
Lincolnwood, IL 60712

Permission is never granted for commercial purposes.

Special thanks to the Campbell's Kitchen and Catherine Marschean-Spivak, Group Manager,
and Jane M. Freiman, Group Manager.

Pictured on the front cover: Broccoli & Cheese Casserole *(page 106)*.

Pictured on the back cover: Japanese Beef Stir-Fry *(page 134)* and Creamy Corn and Vegetable
Orzo *(page 184)*.

ISBN-13: 978-1-60553-182-3
ISBN-10: 1-60553-182-0

Library of Congress Control Number: 2009938230

Manufactured in China.

8 7 6 5 4 3 2 1

Microwave Cooking: Microwave ovens vary in wattage. Use the cooking times as guidelines
and check for doneness before adding more time.

Preparation/Cooking Times: Preparation times are based on the approximate amount
of time required to assemble the recipe before cooking, baking, chilling or serving. These
times include preparation steps such as measuring, chopping and mixing. The fact that some
preparations and cooking can be done simultaneously is taken into account. Preparation of
optional ingredients and serving suggestions is not included.

Publications
International, Ltd.

Contents

Guide for Busy **Cooks**

How many times have you rushed into a grocery store after work at 5:15 p.m., then wandered the aisles wondering what you were going to make for dinner that night? Fact is, we're all busy, and one of the things that seems to get pushed to the back burner as the family schedule starts filling up is meal planning.

Well, sometimes just a shift in thinking, along with a few simple shopping and prep tips, is all you need to make meals a cinch to plan and prepare. Start by planning ahead for a couple of dinners and adjusting the way you shop. Here's what to do when you're at the grocery store:

At the grocery store—

■ Buy a rotisserie chicken. One 2- to 3-pound chicken will yield about 4 cups of shredded meat. Most recipes call for 2 cups—freeze or chill the remaining meat to use in another meal.

■ Purchase twice the amount of meat called for in a recipe. Freeze what you don't use for the night's dinner and plan on using it the following week.

■ When you're at the deli counter stocking up on sliced meat and cheeses for lunches, have the attendant cut small amounts of different varieties of cold cuts, like turkey, salami, and roast beef. Then grab a loaf of artisan bread and plan on panini sandwiches for dinner. (See Fontina Turkey Panini, *page 16*.)

■ Pick up an assortment of fresh bagels— they're not just for breakfast anymore! Use them as an interesting alternative to hamburger buns.

■ Buy frozen meats like fish fillets and boneless, skinless chicken breasts that have been individually frozen. That way, it'll be easy to pull out the quantity you need and leave the rest frozen for another meal.

- Grab a bag of frozen meatballs. You'll be able to get spaghetti and meatballs on the table in record time, but they'll also be the base for hearty meatball sandwiches: Add a jar of *Prego®* Italian Sauce from the pasta aisle, shredded mozzarella, and Parmesan cheese from the dairy case, and a few crusty hoagie buns from the bakery.
- Stock up on resealable plastic bags, freezer bags, and storage containers. They'll come in handy for foods you prepare ahead.
- Buy fresh fruits in season—they make nutritious, ultra-speedy desserts, not to mention that they'll be at the peak of flavor and reasonably priced.

Now that the shopping is done, these prep tips will help you get a jump start on weeknight dinners:

Prepping for the week—

- Brown 2 pounds of ground beef at a time—use one for dinner tonight (see Beef & Bean Burritos, *page 8*, and Southwest Skillet, *page 72*), then package up the remainder in resealable plastic bags or containers and freeze. Now anytime a recipe calls for browned ground beef, you're one step ahead of the game.
- While the ground beef browns, multi-task by pulling the meat off the rotisserie chicken and dividing into 2-cup portions. Freeze in labeled freezer bags or containers and use in soups, stews, or casseroles. (See Spicy Grilled Quesadillas, *page 10*, and Quick Skillet Chicken & Macaroni Parmesan, *page 78*.)
- Hard-cook a few eggs to keep on hand in the refrigerator. They're great for adding protein to salads, or can be made into quick egg salad sandwiches.
- If you're sautéing chicken breasts for dinner, cook a few more, then slice into strips and freeze or chill to add to fajitas, tacos, salads, and pasta dishes. (See Chicken Skillet Fajitas, *page 80*, and Chicken Noodle Casserole, *page 108*.)
- Take a cue from restaurant chefs and chop fresh vegetables like onions, carrots, celery, and bell peppers, packaging them in separate containers or bags in the refrigerator. (Do not freeze—the vegetables will turn mushy.) Making soups, stews, and chilies is so much easier.
- Get in the habit of roasting a bit more beef, pork, or turkey than a recipe calls for—use the extra in sandwiches, pot pies, and pasta dishes. (See Chicken

Broccoli Pockets, *page 35*, and Ham and Broccoli Swirls, *page 136*.)

- If a recipe calls for half a package of pasta, go ahead and cook the full amount and use the remainder in a pasta salad. (See Creamy Corn and Vegetable Orzo, *page 184*, and Tuna & Pasta Cheddar Melt, *page 91*.)
- When meatloaf is on the menu, double the recipe and make meatballs out of the remaining mixture. Brown them off, freeze on a wax paper-lined baking sheet until solid, then package in large resealable plastic bags. You'll be that much closer to spaghetti and meatballs later!
- Wash and spin-dry lettuces, then store in plastic bags lined with paper towels.

If you're going the extra mile and prepping for the week's menu, here's how to store things properly:

- If you've cooked food to be used later or frozen (ground beef, chicken, etc.), wrap it only after it's reached room temperature. Wrapping food while it's still warm can cause harmful bacterial growth. Bring foods to room temperature as quickly as possible by removing them from their cooking vessels and spreading out on baking sheets or pouring into shallow containers. Chill or freeze as soon as they cool down.
- When freezing brothy mixtures like soups and sauces, divide them into storage containers, leaving at least ½ inch at the top of the container to allow for expansion. Let cool to room temperature before freezing.
- Always mark packages clearly with the name of the contents and the date on which it was packaged. Write directly on the bag or on a piece of masking tape on the package using a permanent marker.
- As a rule of thumb, freeze items for no longer than six months; refrigerate for up to three days. Generally speaking, most foods can be frozen without worry— casseroles, soups, stews, and chilies do very well; thaw completely before reheating. Breads, cakes, and cookies freeze well, too. It's best not to freeze fresh vegetables unless they've been cooked briefly (blanched) first. Milk- or dairy-based items, like cream soups and cheese sauces, tend to separate after freezing; this doesn't affect flavor but it does affect appearance. And, never refreeze meat that's already been frozen and thawed—refreezing makes its texture mushy.

Leaving leftovers behind

For the busy cook, leftovers can be extremely helpful in meal planning, giving you a step up on one or two meals for the week. Unfortunately, the busy cook's family isn't always on the same page when it comes to leftovers. Here are a few ideas that are so good, the family may not even know they're getting Tuesday night's roast beef!

■ Make flavorful fajitas by sautéing sliced onion with taco seasoning in a little oil; add strips of leftover roast beef (or chicken), and serve with tortillas, lettuce, cheese, and *Pace*® Picante Sauce.

■ Stir together chunks of leftover roast beef, *Campbell's*® Beef Gravy, and some frozen mixed vegetables. Pour into a greased casserole dish, then top with leftover mashed potatoes or refrigerator biscuits from a can—instant shepherd's pie or pot pie!

■ Sauté sliced onion in oil with Sloppy Joe seasoning mix, then add barbecue sauce and leftover roast beef that you've shredded into strips. Serve on *Pepperidge Farm*® Sesame Rolls for outstanding BBQ beef sandwiches.

Working for the weekend

Time is tight enough during the week— sometimes your best bet for getting a start on dinners for Monday through Friday is to spend a little time on Saturday or Sunday getting your ducks in a row. These ideas can help you do just that:

■ Plan the menu for the week, then shop according to your plan.

■ Chop vegetables, brown ground beef, cook chicken breasts—do anything you can ahead of time, then package, label, and refrigerate or freeze.

■ Wash lettuces for salads; make vinaigrettes and salad dressings.

■ Stir together ingredients for sauces so they're ready to add to dishes.

■ Serve a roast on Sunday, then plan to use the leftovers in a casserole or stew on Tuesday. Or, freeze the leftovers to use later.

■ Prep everything you'll need for a stir-fry—chop onions, peppers, carrots, celery, mushrooms, and meat—and place in individual plastic bags. Store all the small pouches in a larger bag in the refrigerator, and you'll have dinner on the table in about 15 minutes.

20-Minute Dishes

Meals put together in less than

20 minutes, start to finish

Beef & Bean Burritos

Makes 8 burritos

Prep Time: 5 minutes

Cook Time: 15 minutes

Shopping List

ground beef

Bean with Bacon Soup

Chunky Salsa

tortillas

Cheddar cheese

1 pound ground beef

1 can (10 ¾ ounces) Campbell's® Condensed Bean with Bacon Soup

1 cup Pace® Chunky Salsa *or* Pace® Picante Sauce

8 flour tortillas (8-inch), warmed

Shredded Cheddar cheese

Sour cream (optional)

1. Cook the beef in a 10-inch skillet over medium-high heat until it's well browned, stirring often to separate meat. Pour off any fat.

2. Stir the soup and salsa in the skillet and cook until the mixture is hot and bubbling, mashing the beans with a fork.

3. Spoon *about ½ cup* beef mixture down the center of *each* tortilla. Top with the cheese, additional salsa and sour cream, if desired. Fold the tortillas around the filling.

Spicy Grilled Quesadillas

Makes 4 servings

Prep Time: 10 minutes

Cook Time: 5 minutes

Stand Time: 2 minutes

Shopping List

tortillas

Cheddar cheese

Chunky Salsa

chicken

green onions

oil

sour cream

8 flour tortillas (8-inch)

2 cups shredded Cheddar cheese (about 8 ounces)

1 jar (16 ounces) Pace® Chunky Salsa

1 cup diced cooked chicken

4 medium green onions, chopped (about ½ cup)

   Vegetable oil

1 container (8 ounces) sour cream

1. Top **each** of **4** tortillas with ½ **cup** cheese, ¼ **cup** salsa, ¼ **cup** chicken and **2 tablespoons** green onions. Brush the edges of the tortillas with water. Top with the remaining tortillas and press the edges to seal.

2. Lightly oil the grill rack and heat the grill to medium. Brush the tops of the quesadillas with oil. Place the quesadillas, oil-side down, on the grill rack. Brush the other side of the quesadillas with oil. Grill the quesadillas for 5 minutes or until the cheese is melted, turning the quesadillas over once during grilling. Remove the quesadillas from the grill and let stand 2 minutes.

3. Cut the quesadillas into wedges. Serve with the remaining salsa and sour cream.

Kitchen Tip

Quesadillas are an easy way to turn leftover meat and shredded cheese into a whole new meal. You can even combine different varieties of shredded cheese to make the 2 cups needed in this recipe.

Classic Campbelled Eggs

Makes 4 servings

Prep Time: 5 minutes

Cook Time: 15 minutes

Shopping List

Cream of Celery Soup

eggs

butter

parsley

1 can (10 3/4 ounces) Campbell's® Condensed Cream of Celery Soup (Regular *or* 98% Fat Free)

8 eggs

Dash ground black pepper

2 tablespoons butter

Chopped fresh parsley

1. Beat the soup, eggs and black pepper in a medium bowl with a fork or whisk.

2. Heat the butter in a 10-inch skillet over low heat. Add the egg mixture and cook until the eggs are set but still moist. Garnish with the parsley.

Kitchen Tip

*You can substitute **Campbell's**® Condensed Cheddar Cheese Soup for the Cream of Celery.*

Fontina Turkey Panini

Makes 2 sandwiches

Prep Time: 5 minutes

Cook Time: 10 minutes

4 slices Pepperidge Farm® Farmhouse Sourdough Bread

Olive oil

2 tablespoons honey mustard salad dressing

4 slices fontina cheese

2 slices smoked turkey

4 bread-and-butter pickle sandwich slices

1. Brush one side of the bread slices with the oil.

2. Turn *2* bread slices oil-side down. Spread **each** with *1 tablespoon* salad dressing. Top **each** with *2* cheese slices, *1* turkey slice, *2* pickle slices and the remaining bread slices, oil-side up.

3. Heat a grill pan or skillet over medium heat. Add the sandwiches and cook for 4 minutes or until they're lightly browned on both sides and the cheese is melted.

Kitchen Tip

Try pressing down on the sandwiches with a spatula during cooking. It will help the different ingredients melt together.

Shopping List

Farmhouse Sourdough Bread

honey mustard salad dressing

fontina cheese

smoked turkey

pickles

20-Minute Seafood Stew

Makes 4 servings

Prep Time: 5 minutes

Cook Time: 15 minutes

Shopping List

Traditional Italian
Sauce

clam juice

red wine

fish

clams

parsley

2 cups Prego® Traditional Italian Sauce

1 bottle (8 ounces) clam juice

¼ cup Burgundy *or* other dry red wine (optional)

1 pound fresh *or* thawed frozen fish *and/or* shellfish*

8 small clams

Chopped fresh parsley

Use any one or a combination of the following: firm white fish fillets (cut into 2-inch pieces), boneless fish steaks (cut into 1-inch cubes), medium shrimp (peeled and deveined) or scallops.

1. Heat the Italian sauce, clam juice and wine in a 4-quart saucepan over medium heat to a boil. Reduce the heat to low. Cook for 5 minutes.

2. Stir the fish and clams in the saucepan. Cover and cook for 5 minutes or until the fish and clams are done. Garnish with the parsley.

Kitchen Tip

Before cooking, discard any clams that remain open when tapped. After cooking, discard any clams that remain closed.

Fettuccine Picante

Makes 4 servings

½ cup Pace® Picante Sauce

½ cup sour cream

⅓ cup grated Parmesan cheese

½ of a 1-pound package fettuccine, cooked and
    drained

2 tablespoons chopped fresh cilantro leaves

Prep Time: 15 minutes

Cook Time: 5 minutes

1. Heat the picante sauce, sour cream and cheese in
a 2-quart saucepan over medium heat until the mixture
is hot and bubbling.

2. Place the fettuccine and cilantro into a large serving
bowl. Add the mixture and toss to coat. Serve with
additional picante sauce.

Kitchen Tip

*You can use **Pace**® mild, medium or hot Picante
Sauce in this recipe.*

Shopping List

Picante Sauce

sour cream

Parmesan cheese

fettuccine

cilantro

Cheese Steak Pockets

Makes 8 sandwiches

Prep Time: 5 minutes

Cook Time: 10 minutes

1 tablespoon vegetable oil

1 medium onion, sliced

1 package (14 ounces) frozen beef *or* chicken sandwich steaks, separated into 8 portions

1 can ($10^3/_4$ ounces) Campbell's® Condensed Cheddar Cheese Soup

1 jar (about $4^1/_2$ ounces) sliced mushrooms, drained

4 pita breads (6-inch), cut in half

1. Heat the oil in a 10-inch skillet over medium-high heat. Add the onion. Cook and stir until the onion is tender.

2. Add the sandwich steaks and cook until they're browned. Pour off any fat.

3. Add the soup and mushrooms. Reduce the heat to low. Cook and stir until the mixture is hot and bubbling.

4. Divide and spoon the meat mixture into the pita halves.

Shopping List

oil

onion

frozen beef or chicken sandwich steaks

Cheddar Cheese Soup

mushrooms

pita bread

Breakfast Tacos

Makes 2 servings

Prep Time: 10 minutes

Cook Time: 10 minutes

Shopping List

- butter
- potato
- eggs
- bacon
- tortillas
- Cheddar cheese
- Picante Sauce

1 tablespoon butter

1 cup diced cooked potato

4 eggs, beaten

4 slices bacon, cooked and crumbled

4 flour tortillas (8-inch), warmed

$^3/_4$ cup shredded Cheddar cheese

$^1/_2$ cup Pace® Picante Sauce

1. Heat the butter in a 10-inch skillet over medium heat. Add the potato and cook until it's lightly browned, stirring often. Stir in the eggs and bacon and cook until the eggs are set, stirring often.

2. Spoon *about $^1/_2$ cup* potato mixture down the center of *each* tortilla. Divide the cheese and picante sauce evenly among the tortillas. Fold the tortillas around the filling.

Shredded Chicken Soft Tacos

Makes 8 tacos

Prep Time: 5 minutes

Cook Time: 10 minutes

Shopping List

Picante Sauce

chicken

tortillas

guacamole

tomatoes

1 jar (16 ounces) Pace® Picante Sauce

3 cups shredded cooked chicken

8 flour tortillas (8-inch), warmed

   Guacamole

   Chopped tomatoes

   Fresh cilantro leaves (optional)

1. Heat the picante sauce and chicken in a 2-quart saucepan over medium heat until the mixture is hot and bubbling, stirring often.

2. Spoon **about** ⅓ **cup** chicken mixture down the center of **each** tortilla. Top with the guacamole, tomatoes and cilantro, if desired. Fold the tortillas around the filling.

Kitchen Tip

Use store-bought rotisserie chicken or refrigerated cooked chicken strips, shredded, for this recipe.

Picante Skillet Chicken

Makes 6 servings

  1 tablespoon vegetable oil

1¹/₂ pounds skinless, boneless chicken breast halves
     (4 to 6)

  1 jar (16 ounces) Pace® Picante Sauce

  6 cups hot cooked regular long-grain white rice

Prep Time: 5 minutes

Cook Time: 15 minutes

1. Heat the oil in a 10-inch skillet over medium-high heat. Add the chicken and cook for 10 minutes or until it's well browned on both sides.

2. Add the picante sauce to the skillet. Heat to a boil. Reduce the heat to medium. Cover and cook for 5 minutes or until the chicken is cooked through.

3. Serve with the rice.

Shopping List

oil

chicken

Picante Sauce

rice

Italian Sausage Sandwiches

Makes 4 sandwiches

Prep Time: 5 minutes

Cook Time: 15 minutes

1   pound Italian pork sausage, casing removed

1½ cups Prego® Chunky Garden Mushroom & Green Pepper Italian Sauce

4   long hard rolls, split

1. Cook the sausage in a 10-inch skillet over medium-high heat until it's well browned, stirring often to separate meat. Pour off any fat.

2. Stir in the sauce and cook until the mixture is hot and bubbling. Serve the sausage mixture on the rolls.

Kitchen Tip

*You can use your favorite **Prego**® Italian Sauce in this recipe.*

Shopping List

Italian pork sausage

Chunky Garden
Mushroom &
Green Pepper
Italian Sauce

hard rolls

Baked Potatoes Olé

Makes 4 servings

Prep Time: 5 minutes

Cook Time: 15 minutes

1 pound ground beef

1 tablespoon chili powder

1 cup Pace® Picante Sauce

4 hot baked potatoes, split

   Shredded Cheddar cheese

Shopping List

ground beef

chili powder

Picante Sauce

potatoes

Cheddar cheese

1. Cook the beef and chili powder in a 10-inch skillet over medium-high heat until the beef is well browned, stirring often to separate meat. Pour off any fat.

2. Stir the picante sauce in the skillet. Reduce the heat to low. Cook until the mixture is hot and bubbling. Serve the beef mixture over the potatoes. Top with the cheese.

Kitchen Tip

To bake the potatoes, pierce them with a fork and bake at 400°F. for 1 hour or microwave on HIGH for 12 minutes or until fork-tender.

Cheesy Broccoli Potato Topper

Makes 4 servings

Prep Time: 10 minutes

Cook Time: 4 minutes

1 can (10³/₄ ounces) Campbell's® Condensed Cheddar Cheese Soup

4 hot baked potatoes, split

1 cup cooked broccoli flowerets

1. Stir the soup in the can until it's smooth.

2. Place the potatoes onto a microwavable plate. Top with the broccoli. Spoon the soup over the broccoli.

3. Microwave on HIGH for 4 minutes or until the soup is hot.

Shopping List

Cheddar Cheese
Soup

potatoes

broccoli

Quick Chicken Mozzarella Sandwiches

Makes 4 sandwiches

1¹/₂ cups Prego® Three Cheese Italian Sauce

  4 refrigerated *or* thawed frozen cooked breaded
     chicken cutlets

  4 slices mozzarella cheese

  4 round hard rolls

Prep Time: 5 minutes

Cook Time: 15 minutes

1. Heat the sauce in a 10-inch skillet over medium heat to a boil. Place the chicken in the sauce. Reduce the heat to low. Cover and cook for 5 minutes or until the chicken is heated through.

2. Top the chicken with the cheese. Cover and cook until the cheese is melted. Serve on the rolls.

Shopping List

Three Cheese Italian Sauce

breaded chicken cutlets

mozzarella cheese

hard rolls

Apple & Cheddar Bagel Melt Sandwiches

Makes 4 sandwiches

Prep Time: 5 minutes

Broil Time: 2 minutes

$^1/_4$ cup honey

4 Pepperidge Farm® Sesame Bagels, split and toasted **or** Pepperidge Farm® Onion Bagels, split and toasted

1 medium Granny Smith apple, thinly sliced

4 slices Cheddar cheese

Shopping List

honey

Sesame Bagels

Granny Smith apple

Cheddar cheese

1. Heat the broiler. Spread the honey among the bagel halves. Place **4** bagel halves onto a baking sheet and top with the apple and cheese.

2. Broil the bagels with the tops of the bagels 4 inches from the heat for 2 minutes or until the cheese is melted.

3. Top with the remaining bagel halves. Serve immediately.

Kitchen Tip

*Substitute 12 **Pepperidge Farm**® Mini Bagels, any variety, for the regular-size bagels.*

Asian Chicken Stir-Fry

Makes 4 servings

1 tablespoon vegetable oil

1 pound skinless, boneless chicken breasts, cut into strips

1 can (10 3/4 ounces) Campbell's® Condensed Golden Mushroom Soup

3 tablespoons soy sauce

1 teaspoon garlic powder

1 bag (16 ounces) any frozen vegetable combination

   Hot cooked rice

Prep Time: 5 minutes

Cook Time: 15 minutes

1. Heat the oil in a 10-inch skillet over medium-high heat. Add the chicken and stir-fry until it's well browned.

2. Stir the soup, soy sauce and garlic powder into the skillet. Heat to a boil. Add the vegetables. Cook and stir until vegetables are tender-crisp. Serve over the rice.

Shopping List

oil

chicken breasts

Golden Mushroom Soup

soy sauce

garlic powder

frozen vegetable combination

rice

Hearty Ham and Onion Melts

Makes 2 sandwiches

Prep Time: 5 minutes

Cook Time: 15 minutes

Shopping List

red onion

balsamic vinegar

Natural Honey Flax
Bread

deli ham

Muenster cheese

Vegetable cooking spray

1 small red onion, thinly sliced

3 tablespoons balsamic vinegar

4 slices Pepperidge Farm® 100% Natural Honey
Flax Bread

2 ounces deli-sliced reduced-sodium ham

2 ounces sliced Muenster cheese *or* provolone
cheese

1. Spray a 10-inch skillet with the cooking spray and heat over medium heat for 1 minute. Add the onions and cook until they begin to soften. Add the vinegar and cook for 2 minutes or until the onions are tender.

2. Top **2** bread slices with the ham, cheese, onion mixture and remaining bread slices.

3. Spray the skillet with the cooking spray and heat over medium heat for 1 minute. Add the sandwiches and cook until they're lightly browned on both sides and the cheese is melted.

Kitchen Tip

*Also delicious with **Pepperidge Farm**® 100% Natural German Dark Wheat Bread.*

Chicken Broccoli Pockets

Makes 6 sandwiches

1 can (10 3/4 ounces) Campbell's® Healthy Request® Condensed Cream of Chicken Soup

1/4 cup water

1 tablespoon lemon juice

1/4 teaspoon garlic powder

1/8 teaspoon ground black pepper

1 cup cooked broccoli flowerets

1 medium carrot, shredded (about 1/2 cup)

2 cups cubed cooked chicken *or* turkey

3 pita breads (6-inch), cut in half, forming 2 pockets

Prep Time: 15 minutes

Cook Time: 5 minutes

Shopping List
Cream of Chicken Soup
lemon juice
garlic powder
broccoli
carrot
chicken
pita bread

1. Heat all the ingredients, except pita breads, in a 2-quart saucepan over medium heat until the mixture is hot and bubbling.

2. Spoon the chicken mixture into the pita pockets.

Kitchen Tip

This chicken mixture is also delicious served over hot baked potatoes.

Herb Grilled Vegetables

Makes 6 servings

Prep Time: 10 minutes

Cook Time: 10 minutes

Shopping List

Chicken Broth

thyme

red onion

red or green pepper

zucchini or yellow squash

mushrooms

$1/2$ cup Swanson® Natural Goodness® Chicken Broth

$1/2$ teaspoon dried thyme leaves, crushed

$1/8$ teaspoon ground black pepper

1 large red onion, thickly sliced (about 1 cup)

1 large red *or* green pepper, cut into wide strips (about 2 cups)

1 medium zucchini *or* yellow squash, thickly sliced (about $1^1/2$ cups)

2 cups large mushrooms

1. Stir the broth, thyme and black pepper in a small bowl. Brush the vegetables with the broth mixture.

2. Lightly oil the grill rack and heat the grill to medium. Grill the vegetables for 10 minutes or until they're tender-crisp, turning over once during cooking and brushing often with the broth mixture.

Kitchen Tip

A grilling basket is handy for grilling smaller foods like these veggies. Just place the vegetables in a single layer in the basket, close and place on the grill. You can baste the vegetables right in the basket, and flip the basket to grill the other side.

Swanson® Vegetable Broth may be used instead of Swanson® Chicken Broth for a vegetarian dish.

Bruschetta Salad

Makes 6 servings

$^1/_2$ cup olive oil

2 tablespoons red wine vinegar

2 medium tomatoes, cut into 1-inch pieces (about 2 cups)

$^1/_2$ cup thinly sliced cucumber

1 medium red onion, thinly sliced (about $^1/_2$ cup)

$^1/_4$ cup chopped fresh basil leaves

1 tablespoon drained capers

2 cups Pepperidge Farm® Whole Grain Seasoned Croutons

1. Beat the oil and vinegar in a large bowl with a fork or whisk until blended. Add the tomatoes, cucumber, onion, basil and capers and toss to coat. Season to taste.

2. Add the croutons just before serving and toss to coat. Serve immediately.

Kitchen Tip

It's important to serve this salad immediately so that the croutons will stay crisp.

Prep Time: 20 minutes

Shopping List

olive oil

red wine vinegar

tomatoes

cucumber

red onion

basil

capers

Whole Grain Seasoned Croutons

Fabulous Fast Shrimp

Makes 4 servings

Prep Time: 5 minutes

Cook Time: 15 minutes

Shopping List

butter

celery

green pepper

green onions

shrimp

Cream of Chicken Soup

cayenne pepper

rice

paprika

1 tablespoon butter *or* margarine

2 stalks celery, chopped

¼ cup chopped green pepper

¼ cup sliced green onions

1 pound fresh large shrimp, shelled and deveined

1 can (10³/₄ ounces) Campbell's® Condensed Cream of Chicken Soup (Regular *or* 98% Fat Free)

½ cup water

Dash of cayenne pepper

Hot cooked rice

Paprika

1. Heat butter in skillet. Add celery, green pepper and green onions and cook until tender. Add shrimp and cook 3 to 5 minutes or until done.

2. Add soup, water and cayenne pepper and heat through.

3. Serve over rice. Sprinkle with paprika.

4 Ingredients or Less

Just grab a few ingredients and

your dish will be ready in a flash

Grilled Picante BBQ Chicken

Makes 6 servings

Prep Time: 5 minutes

Cook Time: 15 minutes

$^3/_4$ cup Pace® Picante Sauce

$^1/_4$ cup barbecue sauce

6 skinless, boneless chicken breast halves

1. Stir the picante sauce and barbecue sauce in a small bowl. Reserve $^1/_2$ **cup** picante sauce mixture for grilling. Set aside remaining picante sauce mixture to serve with the chicken.

2. Lightly oil the grill rack and heat the grill to medium. Grill the chicken for 15 minutes or until it's cooked through, turning and brushing often with the reserved picante sauce mixture during grilling. Discard any remaining picante sauce mixture.

3. Serve the chicken with the remaining $^1/_2$ **cup** picante sauce mixture.

Shopping List

Picante Sauce

barbecue sauce

chicken

Kitchen Tip

This simple basting sauce also makes a zesty dipping sauce for chicken wings or nuggets.

Pasta Primavera

Makes 4 servings

Prep Time: 5 minutes

Cook Time: 25 minutes

3 cups *uncooked* corkscrew-shaped pasta (rotini)

1 bag (16 ounces) frozen vegetable combination (broccoli, cauliflower, carrots)

1 jar (1 pound 10 ounces) Prego® Traditional Italian Sauce

Grated Parmesan cheese

1. Prepare pasta according to package directions in a 4-quart saucepan. Add the vegetables during the last 5 minutes of the cooking time. Drain the pasta and vegetables in a colander and return them to the saucepan.

2. Stir the Italian sauce into the saucepan. Heat, stirring occasionally, until hot and bubbling. Top with the cheese.

Shopping List

corkscrew-shaped pasta

frozen vegetable combination

Traditional Italian Sauce

Parmesan cheese

Creamy Souper Rice

Makes 4 servings

Prep Time: 5 minutes

Cook Time: 10 minutes

Stand Time: 5 minutes

1 can (10$^3/_4$ ounces) Campbell's® Condensed Cream of Mushroom Soup (Regular *or* 98% Fat Free)

1$^1/_2$ cups Swanson® Natural Goodness® Chicken Broth

1$^1/_2$ cups *uncooked* instant white rice

1 tablespoon grated Parmesan cheese

Freshly ground black pepper

Shopping List

Cream of Mushroom Soup

Chicken Broth

rice

Parmesan cheese

1. Heat the soup and broth in a 2-quart saucepan over medium heat to a boil.

2. Stir the rice and cheese in the saucepan. Cover the saucepan and remove from the heat. Let stand for 5 minutes. Fluff the rice with a fork. Serve with the black pepper and additional Parmesan cheese.

Kitchen Tip

*Any of **Campbell's**® Condensed Cream Soups will work in this recipe: Cream of Chicken, Cream of Celery, even Cheddar Cheese.*

French Onion Burgers

Makes 4 servings

Prep Time: **5 minutes**

Cook Time: **20 minutes**

1 pound ground beef

1 can (10$\frac{1}{2}$ ounces) Campbell's® Condensed French Onion Soup

4 slices Swiss cheese

4 round hard rolls, split

Shopping List

ground beef

French Onion Soup

Swiss cheese

hard rolls

1. Shape the beef into **4** ($\frac{1}{2}$-inch-thick) burgers.

2. Heat a 10-inch skillet over medium-high heat. Add the burgers and cook until they're well browned on both sides. Remove the burgers from the skillet. Pour off any fat.

3. Stir the soup in the skillet and heat to a boil. Return the burgers to the skillet. Reduce the heat to low. Cover and cook for 5 minutes or until the burgers are cooked through. Top the burgers with the cheese and cook until the cheese is melted. Serve the burgers in the rolls with the soup mixture.

Kitchen Tip

You can also serve these burgers in a bowl atop a mound of hot mashed potatoes, with some of the onion gravy poured over.

Sicilian-Style Pizza

Makes 8 servings

Thaw Time: 3 hours

Prep Time: 10 minutes

Bake Time: 25 minutes

2 loaves (1 pound *each*) frozen white bread dough

   Vegetable cooking spray

1³/₄ cups Prego® Traditional Italian Sauce

2 cups shredded mozzarella cheese
   (about 8 ounces)

Shopping List

frozen white bread dough

Traditional Italian Sauce

mozzarella cheese

1. Thaw the bread dough according to the package directions. Heat the oven to 375°F. Spray a 15×10-inch jellyroll pan with cooking spray. Place the dough loaves into the pan. Press the dough from the center out until it covers the bottom of the pan. Pinch the edges of the dough to form a rim.

2. Spread the sauce over the crust. Top with the cheese.

3. Bake for 25 minutes or until the cheese is melted and the crust is golden.

Kitchen Tip

To thaw the dough more quickly, place the dough into a microwavable dish. Brush with melted butter or spray with vegetable cooking spray. Microwave on LOW for 1 to 2 minutes.

Chocolate Goldfish® Pretzel Clusters

Makes 1 pound

Prep Time: 5 minutes

Cook Time: 1 minute

Chill Time: 30 minutes

1 package (12 ounces) semi-sweet chocolate pieces (about 2 cups)

2½ cups Pepperidge Farm® Pretzel Goldfish® Crackers

1 container (4 ounces) multi-colored nonpareils

Shopping List

semi-sweet chocolate pieces

Pretzel Goldfish Crackers

nonpareils

1. Line a baking sheet with waxed paper. Place the chocolate into a microwavable bowl. Microwave on HIGH for 1 minute. Stir. Microwave at 15-second intervals, stirring after each, until the chocolate is melted and smooth. Add the Goldfish® crackers and stir to coat.

2. Drop the chocolate mixture by tablespoonfuls onto the baking sheet. Sprinkle the clusters with the nonpareils.

3. Refrigerate for 30 minutes or until the clusters are firm. Store in the refrigerator.

Kitchen Tip

To wrap for gift-giving, arrange the clusters in small candy box lined with colored plastic wrap.

Grilled Beef Steak with Sauteéd Onions

Makes 8 servings

Prep Time: 10 minutes

Cook Time: 5 minutes

Grill Time: 20 minutes

Stand Time: 5 minutes

2 tablespoons olive oil

2 large onions, thinly sliced (about 2 cups)

1 jar (16 ounces) Pace® Chunky Salsa

  2-pound boneless beef sirloin steak, strip steak *or* rib steak

1. Heat **1 tablespoon** oil in a 12-inch skillet over medium heat. Add the onions and cook until they're tender. Add **2½ cups** salsa and cook until heated through. Remove the onion mixture from the skillet and keep warm.

2. Lightly oil the grill rack and heat the grill to medium. Grill the steak for 20 minutes for medium-rare or to desired doneness, turning the steak over halfway through cooking and brushing often with remaining salsa. Discard any leftover salsa.

3. Let steak stand 5 minutes then cut into **8** pieces. Serve with the onion mixture.

Kitchen Tip

This recipe will work fine with almost any kind of onion.

Shopping List

olive oil

onions

Chunky Salsa

steak

Italian Cheeseburger Pasta

Makes 4 servings

Prep Time: 5 minutes

Cook Time: 35 minutes

1 pound ground beef

1 jar (1 pound 10 ounces) Prego® Traditional Italian Sauce

2 cups water

2 cups *uncooked* corkscrew-shaped pasta (rotini)

$1/2$ cup shredded mozzarella cheese

1. Cook the beef in a 10-inch skillet over medium-high heat until well browned, stirring frequently to separate meat. Pour off any fat.

2. Stir the Italian sauce, water and pasta into the skillet. Heat to a boil. Reduce the heat to medium. Cook and stir for 25 minutes or until the pasta is tender but still firm. Sprinkle with the cheese.

Shopping List

ground beef

Traditional Italian
Sauce

corkscrew-shaped
pasta

mozzarella cheese

Polenta au Gratin

Makes 6 servings

Prep Time: 10 minutes

Bake Time: 25 minutes

Stand Time: 5 minutes

1 cup Pace® Picante Sauce

1 package (18 ounces) prepared polenta, cut into $1/2$-inch slices

4 green onions, minced (about $1/2$ cup)

$1^1/_2$ cups shredded Mexican cheese blend (about 6 ounces)

Shopping List

Picante Sauce

polenta

green onions

Mexican cheese blend

1. Heat the oven to 350°F. Spread *$1/2$ cup* picante sauce on the bottom of a 2-quart shallow baking dish. Layer the polenta slices, overlapping slightly, in the baking dish. Top with the green onions, remaining picante sauce and cheese.

2. Bake for 25 minutes or until the polenta is golden brown and the cheese is melted. Let stand for 5 minutes.

Sirloin Steak Picante

Makes 6 servings

Prep Time: **5 minutes**

Grill Time: **22 minutes**

Stand Time: **10 minutes**

Shopping List

steak

Picante Sauce

1½ pounds boneless beef sirloin **or** top round steak, 1½-inch thick

1 cup Pace® Picante Sauce **or** Chunky Salsa

1. Lightly oil the grill rack and heat the grill to medium.

2. Grill the steak for 25 minutes for medium or to desired doneness, turning the steak over once during grilling and brushing often with ½ **cup** of the picante sauce. Discard any remaining picante sauce mixture.

3. Slice the steak and serve with the remaining ½ **cup** picante sauce.

Kitchen Tip

The picante sauce keeps the meat moist during grilling and adds tons of flavor. Vary the heat level using the mild, medium or hot varieties.

2-Step Nacho Pasta

Makes 4 servings

Prep Time: 5 minutes

Cook Time: 20 minutes

Shopping List

Fiesta Nacho Cheese
Soup

milk

corkscrew-shaped
pasta

1 can (11 ounces) Campbell's® Condensed Fiesta Nacho Cheese Soup

¹/₂ cup milk

4 cups corkscrew-shaped pasta (rotini), cooked and drained

1. Heat the soup and milk in a 2-quart saucepan over medium heat. Cook until hot and bubbling.

2. Stir in the pasta. Cook and stir until hot.

Pizza Fries

Makes 8 servings

1 bag (2 pounds) frozen French fries

1 cup Prego® Traditional Italian Sauce, any variety

1¹/₂ cups shredded mozzarella cheese
(about 6 ounces)

Diced pepperoni (optional)

Prep Time: 20 minutes

Bake Time: 5 minutes

1. Prepare the fries according to the package directions. Remove from the oven. Pour the sauce over the fries.

2. Top with the cheese and pepperoni, if desired.

3. Bake for 5 minutes or until the cheese is melted.

Shopping List

French fries

Traditional Italian
Sauce

mozzarella cheese

Power Breakfast Sandwiches

Makes 2 sandwiches

Prep Time: 5 minutes

$\frac{1}{4}$ cup peanut butter

4 slices Pepperidge Farm® 100% Natural 100% Whole Wheat Bread

$\frac{1}{4}$ cup raisins

1 medium banana, sliced

Shopping List

peanut butter

Whole Wheat Bread

raisins

banana

Spread the peanut butter on **4** bread slices. Divide the raisins and banana between **2** bread slices. Top with the remaining bread slices, peanut butter-side down. Cut the sandwiches in half.

Kitchen Tip

Substitute 1 large apple, cored and sliced, for the raisins and banana.

Cheeseburger Pasta

Makes 5 servings

1 pound ground beef

1 can (10³/₄ ounces) Campbell's® Condensed Cheddar Cheese Soup

1 can (10³/₄ ounces) Campbell's® Condensed Tomato Soup (Regular *or* Healthy Request®)

1½ cups water

2 cups *uncooked* medium shell-shaped pasta

Prep Time: **5 minutes**

Cook Time: **20 minutes**

1. Cook the beef in a 10-inch skillet over medium-high heat until it's well browned, stirring often to separate meat. Pour off any fat.

2. Stir the soups, water and pasta in the skillet and heat to a boil. Reduce the heat to medium. Cook for 10 minutes or until the pasta is tender, stirring often.

Shopping List

ground beef

Cheddar Cheese Soup

Tomato Soup

shell-shaped pasta

Sloppy Joes Italiano

Makes 6 servings

Prep Time: 5 minutes

Cook Time: 15 minutes

Shopping List

ground beef

Italian Sauce

Parmesan cheese

hamburger rolls

1 pound ground beef

2 cups Prego® Italian Sauce, any variety

¼ cup grated Parmesan cheese

6 hamburger rolls, split

1. Cook the beef in a 10-inch skillet over medium-high heat until the beef is well browned, stirring frequently to separate meat. Pour off any fat.

2. Stir the sauce and cheese into the skillet. Cook until the mixture is hot and bubbling.

3. Divide the beef mixture among the rolls.

Easy Beef & Pasta

Makes 4 servings

1 tablespoon vegetable oil

1 pound boneless beef sirloin steak, $^3/_4$-inch thick, cut into very thin strips

1 can (10$^3/_4$ ounces) Campbell's® Condensed Tomato Soup (Regular *or* Healthy Request®)

$^1/_2$ cup water

1 bag (about 16 ounces) frozen vegetable pasta blend

Prep Time: 5 minutes

Cook Time: 20 minutes

1. Heat the oil in a 10-inch skillet over medium-high heat. Add the beef and cook until it's well browned, stirring often. Pour off any fat.

2. Stir the soup, water and vegetable pasta blend in the skillet and heat to a boil. Reduce the heat to low. Cover and cook for 5 minutes or until the beef is cooked through.

Shopping List

oil

sirloin steak

Tomato Soup

frozen vegetable pasta blend

Easy *Skillets*

Bring out your skillet for a quick

and easy dinner

Chicken Pesto with Tomatoes

Makes 4 servings

Prep Time: **5 minutes**

Cook Time: **20 minutes**

Shopping List

chicken

Cream of Chicken
Soup

pesto sauce

canned tomatoes

Vegetable cooking spray

4 skinless, boneless chicken breast halves

1 can (10 ¾ ounces) Campbell's® Condensed Cream
of Chicken Soup (Regular *or* 98% Fat Free)

½ cup water

⅓ cup prepared pesto sauce

1 can (about 14.5 ounces) diced tomatoes,
undrained

Hot cooked pasta (optional)

1. Spray a 10-inch skillet with the cooking spray and heat over medium-high heat for 1 minute. Add the chicken and cook for 10 minutes or until it's well browned on both sides. Remove the chicken from the skillet.

2. Stir the soup, water, pesto and tomatoes in the skillet and heat to a boil. Return the chicken to the skillet. Reduce the heat to low. Cover and cook for 5 minutes or until the chicken is cooked through. Serve with the pasta, if desired.

Beef Stroganoff

Makes 4 servings

Prep Time: 10 minutes

Cook Time: 25 minutes

1 tablespoon vegetable oil

1 pound boneless beef sirloin steak *or* beef top round steak, $3/4$-inch thick, cut into thin strips

1 medium onion, chopped (about $1/2$ cup)

1 can (10 $3/4$ ounces) Campbell's® Condensed Cream of Mushroom Soup (Regular, 98% Fat Free *or* Healthy Request®)

$1/2$ teaspoon paprika

$1/3$ cup sour cream *or* plain yogurt

4 cups hot cooked whole wheat *or* regular egg noodles

Chopped fresh parsley

1. Heat the oil in a 12-inch nonstick skillet over medium-high heat. Add the beef and cook until it's well browned, stirring often. Remove the beef from the skillet. Pour off any fat.

2. Reduce the heat to medium. Add the onion to the skillet and cook until it's tender.

3. Stir the soup and paprika in the skillet and heat to a boil. Stir in the sour cream. Return the beef to the skillet and cook until the mixture is hot and bubbling. Serve the beef mixture over the noodles. Sprinkle with the parsley.

Shopping List

oil

steak

onion

Cream of Mushroom Soup

paprika

sour cream

egg noodles

parsley

Southwest Skillet

Makes 4 servings

Prep Time: 5 minutes

Cook Time: 20 minutes

Stand Time: 5 minutes

$3/4$ pound ground beef

1 tablespoon chili powder

1 can (10 $3/4$ ounces) Campbell's® Condensed Beefy Mushroom Soup

$1/4$ cup water

1 can (14.5 ounces) whole peeled tomatoes, cut up

1 can (about 15 ounces) kidney beans, rinsed and drained

$3/4$ cup *uncooked* instant rice

$1/2$ cup shredded Cheddar cheese (2 ounces)

Crumbled tortilla chips

1. Cook the beef with chili powder in a 10-inch skillet over medium-high heat until the beef is well browned, stirring frequently to separate meat. Pour off any fat.

2. Stir the soup, water, tomatoes and beans into the skillet. Heat to a boil. Reduce the heat to low. Cover and cook for 10 minutes.

3. Stir the rice into the skillet. Cover the skillet and remove from heat. Let stand 5 minutes. Top with the cheese. Serve with the chips.

Shopping List

ground beef

chili powder

Beefy Mushroom Soup

canned tomatoes

kidney beans

rice

Cheddar cheese

tortilla chips

Rosemary Chicken & Mushroom Pasta

Makes 6 servings

Prep Time: 10 minutes

Cook Time: 20 minutes

2 tablespoons olive *or* vegetable oil

$1^{1}/_{2}$ pounds skinless, boneless chicken breasts, cut into strips

4 cups sliced mushrooms (about 12 ounces)

1 tablespoon minced garlic

1 tablespoon chopped fresh rosemary leaves *or* 1 teaspoon dried rosemary leaves, crushed

1 can (14 $^{1}/_{2}$ ounces) Campbell's® Chicken Gravy

1 package (1 pound) linguine *or* spaghetti, cooked and drained

Shredded Parmesan cheese

1. Heat the oil in a 12-inch skillet over medium-high heat. Add the chicken and mushrooms in 2 batches and cook until the chicken is well browned, stirring often. Remove the chicken mixture from the skillet.

2. Reduce the heat to low. Stir the garlic and rosemary in the skillet and cook for 1 minute. Stir the gravy in the skillet and heat to a boil.

3. Return the chicken and mushrooms to the skillet. Cover and cook for 5 minutes or until the chicken is cooked through. Place the pasta in a large serving bowl. Pour the chicken mixture over the pasta. Toss to coat. Serve with the cheese.

Shopping List

olive oil

chicken

mushrooms

garlic

rosemary

Chicken Gravy

linguine

Parmesan cheese

Kitchen Tip

For a rustic twist, try whole wheat pasta in the recipe.

Steak & Mushroom Florentine

Makes 4 servings

Prep Time: 5 minutes

Cook Time: 20 minutes

2 tablespoons vegetable oil

1 pound beef sirloin steak *or* beef top round steak, $3/4$-inch thick, cut into thin strips

1 small onion, sliced (about $1/4$ cup)

4 cups fresh baby spinach leaves

1 can (10 $3/4$ ounces) Campbell's® Condensed Cream of Mushroom Soup (Regular *or* 98% Fat Free)

1 cup water

1 large tomato, thickly sliced

Freshly ground black pepper

1. Heat *1 tablespoon* oil in a 10-inch skillet over medium-high heat. Add the beef and cook until it's well browned, stirring often. Remove the beef from the skillet. Pour off any fat.

2. Reduce the heat to medium. Add the remaining oil to the skillet. Add the onion and cook until it's tender-crisp. Add the spinach and cook until the spinach is wilted.

3. Stir the soup and water in the skillet and heat to a boil. Return the beef to the skillet. Reduce the heat to low. Cook until the mixture is hot and bubbling. Serve the beef mixture over the tomato. Season with the black pepper.

Shopping List

oil

steak

onion

spinach

Cream of Mushroom Soup

tomato

Quick Skillet Chicken & Macaroni Parmesan

Makes 6 servings

Prep Time: 15 minutes
Cook Time: 15 minutes
Stand Time: 5 minutes

Shopping List

Traditional Italian Sauce

Parmesan cheese

chicken

elbow macaroni

mozzarella cheese

1 jar (1 pound 10 ounces) Prego® Traditional Italian Sauce *or* Prego® Organic Tomato & Basil Italian Sauce

¼ cup grated Parmesan cheese

3 cups cubed cooked chicken

1½ cups elbow macaroni, cooked and drained

1½ cups shredded part-skim mozzarella cheese (6 ounces)

1. Heat the Italian sauce, **3 tablespoons** of the Parmesan cheese, chicken and macaroni in a 10-inch skillet over medium-high heat to a boil. Reduce the heat to medium. Cover and cook for 10 minutes or until the mixture is hot and bubbling, stirring occasionally.

2. Sprinkle with the mozzarella cheese and remaining Parmesan cheese. Let stand for 5 minutes or until the cheese melts.

Kitchen Tip

Use 1½ pounds skinless, boneless chicken breasts, cut into cubes for the cooked chicken. Heat 1 tablespoon olive oil in a 12-inch skillet over medium-high heat. Add the chicken in 2 batches and cook until it's well browned, stirring often. Continue to cook, proceeding as directed in step 1 above.

Chicken Skillet Fajitas

Makes 8 fajitas

Prep Time: 10 minutes

Cook Time: 20 minutes

1 tablespoon vegetable oil

1 pound skinless, boneless chicken breast halves, cut into strips

1 large green pepper, cut into 2-inch-long strips (about 2 cups)

1 large onion, sliced (about 1 cup)

1 can (10 $^3/_4$ ounces) Campbell's® Condensed Cream of Chicken Soup (Regular **or** 98% Fat Free)

$^1/_2$ teaspoon ground cumin

$^1/_2$ teaspoon chili powder

$^1/_4$ teaspoon garlic powder

8 flour tortillas (8-inch), warmed

1. Heat the oil in a 10-inch skillet over medium-high heat. Add the chicken and cook until it's well browned, stirring often.

2. Reduce the heat to medium. Add the pepper and onion and cook until they're tender. Stir the soup, cumin, chili and garlic powders into the skillet. Cook until the mixture is hot and bubbling.

3. Spoon **about $^1/_3$ cup** of the chicken mixture down the center of **each** tortilla. Fold the tortilla over the filling.

Shopping List

oil

chicken

green pepper

onion

Cream of Chicken Soup

cumin

chili powder

garlic powder

tortillas

Kitchen Tip

To warm the tortillas you may either wrap them in damp paper towels and microwave on HIGH for about 1 minute or wrap in foil and bake.

Skillet Vegetable Lasagna

Makes 4 servings

Prep Time: 10 minutes

Cook Time: 15 minutes

1 3/4 cups Swanson® Vegetable Broth (Regular *or* Certified Organic)

2/3 of a 1-pound package of *uncooked* oven-ready (no-boil) lasagna noodles (about 15)

1 can (10 3/4 ounces) Campbell's® Condensed Cream of Mushroom Soup (Regular *or* 98% Fat Free)

1 can (about 14.5 ounces) diced tomatoes, undrained

1 package (10 ounces) frozen chopped spinach, thawed and well drained

1 cup ricotta cheese

1 cup shredded mozzarella cheese (about 4 ounces)

1. Heat the broth in a 12-inch skillet over medium-high heat to a boil. Break the noodles into pieces and add to the broth. Reduce the heat to low. Cook for 3 minutes or until the noodles are tender.

2. Stir the soup, tomatoes and spinach in the skillet. Cook for 5 minutes or until the mixture is hot and bubbling.

3. Remove the skillet from the heat. Spoon the ricotta cheese on top and sprinkle with the mozzarella cheese.

Kitchen Tip

You can try using 4 ounces mozzarella, cut into very thin slices, instead of the shredded mozzarella.

Shopping List

Vegetable Broth

lasagna noodles

Cream of Mushroom Soup

tomatoes

spinach

ricotta cheese

mozzarella cheese

Quick & Easy Chicken, Broccoli & Brown Rice Dinner

Makes 4 servings

Prep Time: 5 minutes

Cook Time: 20 minutes

1 tablespoon vegetable oil

4 skinless, boneless chicken breast halves

1 can (10 ¾ ounces) Campbell's® Condensed Cream of Chicken Soup (Regular, 98% Fat Free *or* Healthy Request®)

1½ cups water

¼ teaspoon paprika

¼ teaspoon ground black pepper

1½ cups *uncooked* instant brown rice*

2 cups fresh *or* frozen broccoli flowerets

Cooking times vary. To insure best results, use instant whole grain brown rice.

1. Heat the oil in a 10-inch skillet over medium-high heat. Add the chicken and cook for 10 minutes or until it's well browned on both sides. Remove the chicken from the skillet.

2. Stir the soup, water, paprika and black pepper in the skillet and heat to a boil.

3. Stir the rice and broccoli in the skillet. Reduce the heat to low. Return the chicken to the skillet. Sprinkle the chicken with additional paprika and black pepper. Cover and cook for 5 minutes or until the chicken is cooked through and the rice is tender.

Shopping List

oil

chicken

Cream of Chicken Soup

paprika

brown rice

broccoli

Crusted Tilapia Florentine

Makes 4 servings

Prep Time: 10 minutes

Cook Time: 15 minutes

1 egg

2 teaspoons water

1 cup Italian-seasoned dry bread crumbs

4 fresh tilapia fillets (about 4 ounces *each*)

2 tablespoons olive oil

2 2/3 cups Prego® Traditional Italian Sauce

2 cups frozen chopped spinach

Hot cooked noodles

Shopping List

egg

bread crumbs

tilapia

olive oil

Traditional Italian Sauce

spinach

noodles

1. Beat the egg and water with a fork in a shallow dish. Place the bread crumbs on a plate. Dip the fish in the egg mixture, then coat with the bread crumbs.

2. Heat the oil in a 12-inch skillet over medium-high heat. Add the fish and cook for 8 minutes, turning once or until the fish flakes easily when tested with a fork. Remove the fish and keep warm.

3. Stir the Italian sauce and spinach into the skillet. Heat to a boil. Reduce the heat to medium. Cook for 2 minutes or until the spinach is wilted. Serve the sauce over the fish. Serve with the noodles.

Simple Salisbury Steaks

Makes 4 servings

Prep Time: 15 minutes

Cook Time: 25 minutes

1 can (10³/₄ ounces) Campbell's® Condensed Cream of Mushroom Soup (Regular *or* 98% Fat Free)

1 pound ground beef

¹/₃ cup dry bread crumbs

1 small onion, finely chopped (about ¹/₄ cup)

1 egg, beaten

1 tablespoon vegetable oil

1¹/₂ cups sliced mushrooms (about 4 ounces)

1. Thoroughly mix **¹/₄ cup** soup, beef, bread crumbs, onion and egg in a large bowl. Shape **firmly** into **4** (¹/₂-inch-thick) patties.

2. Heat the oil in a 10-inch skillet over medium-high heat. Add the patties and cook until they're well browned on both sides. Pour off any fat.

3. Add the remaining soup and mushrooms to the skillet and heat to a boil. Reduce the heat to low. Cover and cook for 10 minutes or until the patties are cooked through.

Shopping List

Cream of Mushroom Soup

ground beef

bread crumbs

onion

egg

oil

mushrooms

Skillet Fiesta Chicken & Rice

Makes 4 servings

1 tablespoon vegetable oil

4 skinless, boneless chicken breast halves

1 can (10¾ ounces) Campbell's® Condensed Tomato Soup (Regular *or* Healthy Request®)

1⅓ cups water

1 teaspoon chili powder

1½ cups *uncooked* instant white rice

¼ cup shredded Cheddar cheese

Prep Time: 5 minutes

Cook Time: 20 minutes

Shopping List

oil

chicken

Tomato Soup

chili powder

rice

Cheddar cheese

1. Heat the oil in a 10-inch skillet over medium-high heat. Add the chicken and cook for 10 minutes or until it's well browned on both sides. Remove the chicken from the skillet.

2. Stir the soup, water and chili powder in the skillet and heat to a boil.

3. Stir in the rice. Place the chicken on the rice mixture. Sprinkle the chicken with additional chili powder and the cheese. Reduce the heat to low. Cover and cook for 5 minutes or until the chicken is cooked through and the rice is tender. Stir the rice mixture before serving.

Kitchen Tip

Try Mexican-blend shredded cheese instead of the Cheddar if you like.

Chicken & Roasted Garlic Risotto

Makes 4 servings

Prep Time: 5 minutes

Cook Time: 20 minutes

Stand Time: 5 minutes

Shopping List

chicken

butter

Cream of Chicken Soup

Cream of Mushroom with Roasted Garlic Soup

rice

peas and carrots

4   skinless, boneless chicken breast halves

1   tablespoon butter

1   can (10 $3/4$ ounces) Campbell's® Condensed Cream of Chicken Soup (Regular *or* 98% Fat Free)

1   can (10 $3/4$ ounces) Campbell's® Condensed Cream of Mushroom with Roasted Garlic Soup

2   cups water

2   cups *uncooked* instant white rice

1   cup frozen peas and carrots

1. Season the chicken as desired.

2. Heat the butter in a 10-inch skillet over medium-high heat. Add the chicken and cook for 10 minutes or until it's well browned on both sides. Remove the chicken from the skillet.

3. Stir the soups and water in the skillet and heat to a boil. Stir in the rice and vegetables. Return the chicken to the skillet. Reduce the heat to low. Cover and cook for 5 minutes or until the chicken is cooked through. Remove the skillet from the heat. Let stand for 5 minutes.

Kitchen Tip

Traditionally, risotto is made by sautéing rice in butter then stirring broth into the rice a little at a time—very labor-intensive. This dish gives you the same creamy texture with a lot less work!

Tuna & Pasta Cheddar Melt

Makes 4 servings

1 can (10 1/2 ounces) Campbell's® Condensed Chicken Broth

1 soup can water

1/2 of a 1-pound package *uncooked* corkscrew-shaped pasta (rotini) (about 3 cups)

1 can (10 3/4 ounces) Campbell's® Condensed Cream of Mushroom Soup (Regular *or* 98% Fat Free)

1 cup milk

1 can (about 6 ounces) tuna, drained and flaked

1 cup shredded Cheddar cheese (about 4 ounces)

2 tablespoons Italian-seasoned dry bread crumbs

2 teaspoons butter or margarine, melted

1. Heat the broth and the water to a boil over medium-high heat in a large skillet. Add the pasta and cook until it's just tender, stirring often. Do not drain.

2. Stir the soup, milk and tuna in the skillet. Top with the cheese. Mix the bread crumbs with the butter. Sprinkle on top. Heat through.

Prep Time: 10 minutes

Cook Time: 15 minutes

Shopping List

Chicken Broth

corkscrew-shaped pasta

Cream of Mushroom Soup

milk

tuna

Cheddar cheese

bread crumbs

butter

Beef Stir-Fry

Makes 4 servings

Prep Time: 10 minutes

Cook Time: 25 minutes

2 tablespoons cornstarch

1 can (10 1/2 ounces) Campbell's® Condensed Beef Broth

2 tablespoons soy sauce

2 tablespoons vegetable oil

1 pound boneless beef sirloin *or* top round steak, 3/4-inch thick, cut into thin strips

3 cups cut-up vegetables (broccoli flowerets, sliced carrots and green *or* red pepper strips

1/4 teaspoon garlic powder *or* 1 clove garlic, minced

Hot cooked rice

Shopping List

cornstarch

Beef Broth

soy sauce

oil

steak

vegetables

garlic powder

rice

1. Stir the cornstarch, broth and soy sauce in a small bowl until smooth. Set aside.

2. Heat the oil in a 10-inch skillet. Add the beef and stir-fry until it's well browned and the juices evaporate. Push the beef to one side of the skillet.

3. Add the vegetables and garlic powder and stir-fry until tender-crisp.

4. Stir the cornstarch mixture and stir into the skillet. Cook and stir until the mixture boils and thickens. Serve over the rice.

Chicken Scampi

Makes 4 servings

2 tablespoons butter

4 skinless, boneless chicken breast halves

1 can (10 3/4 ounces) Campbell's® Condensed Cream
   of Chicken Soup (Regular *or* 98% Fat Free)

1/4 cup water

2 teaspoons lemon juice

2 cloves garlic, minced *or* 1/2 teaspoon garlic powder

   Hot cooked pasta

Prep Time: 5 minutes

Cook Time: 20 minutes

1. Heat the butter in a 10-inch skillet over medium-high heat. Add the chicken and cook for 10 minutes or until it's well browned on both sides. Remove the chicken and set aside.

2. Stir the soup, water, lemon juice and garlic into the skillet. Heat to a boil. Return the chicken to the skillet and reduce the heat to low. Cover and cook for 5 minutes or until chicken is cooked through.

3. Serve with the pasta.

Shopping List

butter

chicken

Cream of Chicken
Soup

lemon juice

garlic

pasta

Spicy Salsa Mac & Beef

Makes 4 servings

Prep Time: 5 minutes

Cook Time: 20 minutes

1 pound ground beef

1 can (10$^{1}/_{2}$ ounces) Campbell's® Condensed Beef Broth

1$^{1}/_{3}$ cups water

2 cups *uncooked* medium shell-shaped pasta

1 can (10$^{3}/_{4}$ ounces) Campbell's® Condensed Cheddar Cheese Soup

1 cup chunky salsa

Shopping List

ground beef

Beef Broth

shell-shaped pasta

Cheddar Cheese Soup

chunky salsa

1. Cook the beef in a 10-inch skillet over medium-high heat until the beef is well browned, stirring frequently to separate meat. Pour off any fat.

2. Stir the broth and water into the skillet. Heat to a boil. Add the pasta. Reduce the heat to medium. Cook and stir for 10 minutes or until the pasta is tender but still firm.

3. Stir the soup and salsa into the skillet. Cook and stir until hot and bubbling.

Autumn Pork Chops

Makes 4 servings

1 tablespoon vegetable oil

4 bone-in pork chops, ½-inch thick (about 1 pound)

1 can (10 ¾ ounces) Campbell's® Condensed Cream of Celery Soup (Regular *or* 98% Fat Free)

½ cup apple juice *or* water

2 tablespoons spicy-brown mustard

1 tablespoon honey

Generous dash ground black pepper

Hot cooked medium egg noodles

Prep Time: 5 minutes

Cook Time: 20 minutes

Shopping List

oil

pork chops

Cream of Celery Soup

apple juice

spicy mustard

honey

egg noodles

1. Heat the oil in a 10-inch skillet over medium-high heat. Add the pork chops and cook until the chops are well browned on both sides. Remove the pork chops and set aside.

2. Stir the soup, apple juice, mustard, honey and black pepper into the skillet. Heat to a boil. Return the pork chops to the skillet and reduce the heat to low. Cover and cook for 5 minutes or until the chops are cooked through.

3. Serve with the noodles.

Easy Chicken and Pasta

Makes 4 servings

Prep Time: 5 minutes

Cook Time: 25 minutes

1   tablespoon vegetable oil

4   skinless, boneless chicken breasts, cut into 1-inch pieces

1   can (10 $\frac{3}{4}$ ounces) Campbell's® Condensed Cream of Mushroom Soup (Regular *or* 98% Fat Free)

2 $\frac{1}{4}$ cups water

$\frac{1}{2}$ teaspoon dried basil leaves, crushed

2   cups frozen vegetable combination (broccoli, cauliflower, carrots)

2   cups *uncooked* corkscrew-shaped pasta (rotini)

Grated Parmesan cheese

Shopping List

oil

chicken

Cream of Mushroom Soup

basil

frozen vegetable combination

corkscrew-shaped pasta

Parmesan cheese

1. Heat the oil in a 10-inch skillet over medium-high heat. Add the chicken and cook until it's well browned, stirring often. Remove the chicken with a slotted spoon and set aside.

2. Stir the soup, water, basil and vegetables into the skillet. Heat to a boil. Add the pasta. Reduce the heat to medium. Cook and stir for 10 minutes.

3. Return the chicken to the skillet. Cook for 5 minutes more or until the pasta is tender but still firm. Sprinkle with the cheese.

Beef Taco Skillet

Makes 4 servings

1 pound ground beef

1 can (10 ³/₄ ounces) Campbell's® Condensed Tomato Soup (Regular *or* Healthy Request®)

¹/₂ cup salsa

¹/₂ cup water

6 flour tortillas (6-inch), cut into 1-inch pieces

¹/₂ cup shredded Cheddar cheese

Prep Time: 5 minutes

Cook Time: 20 minutes

1. Cook the beef in a 10-inch skillet over medium-high heat until it's well browned, stirring often to separate meat. Pour off any fat.

2. Stir the soup, salsa, water and tortillas in the skillet and heat to a boil. Reduce the heat to low. Cook for 5 minutes. Stir the beef mixture. Top with the cheese.

Shopping List

ground beef

Tomato Soup

salsa

tortillas

Cheddar cheese

Fish & Vegetable Skillet

Makes 4 servings

Prep Time: 15 minutes

Cook Time: 15 minutes

Shopping List

thyme

carrot

celery

onion

Cream of Mushroom
Soup

fish fillets

$1/4$ cup water

2 tablespoons dry white wine (optional)

$1/2$ teaspoon dried thyme leaves, crushed

Generous dash ground black pepper

1 large carrot, cut into matchstick-thin strips
(about 1 cup)

2 stalks celery, cut into matchstick-thin strips
(about $1\,1/3$ cups)

1 small onion, chopped (about $1/4$ cup)

1 can (10 $3/4$ ounces) Campbell's® Cream of
Mushroom Soup (Regular *or* Healthy Request®)

1 pound firm white fish fillets (cod, haddock *or*
halibut)

1. Heat the water, wine, thyme, black pepper, carrot,
celery and onion in a 10-inch skillet over medium heat
to a boil. Reduce the heat to low. Cover and cook for
5 minutes or until the vegetables are tender-crisp.

2. Stir the soup in the
skillet. Top with the fish.
Cover and cook for
5 minutes or until the fish
flakes easily when tested
with a fork.

Beef & Rice Taco Casserole

Makes 4 servings

Prep Time: 10 minutes

Bake Time: 25 minutes

Shopping List

ground beef

Tomato Soup

Chunky Salsa

milk

rice

tortilla chips

Cheddar cheese

1 pound ground beef

1 can (10 ¾ ounces) Campbell's® Condensed Tomato Soup

1 cup Pace® Chunky Salsa *or* Picante Sauce

½ cup milk

½ cup **uncooked** instant white rice

½ cup crushed tortilla chips

½ cup shredded Cheddar cheese

1. Cook the beef in a 10-inch skillet over medium-high heat until the beef is well browned, stirring frequently to separate meat. Pour off any fat.

2. Stir the soup, salsa, milk and rice into the skillet. Spoon the soup mixture into a 1½-quart casserole. Cover the dish with foil.

3. Bake at 400°F. for 25 minutes or until hot. Stir.

4. Sprinkle the chips around the edge of the casserole. Sprinkle with the cheese.

Homestyle Chicken & Biscuits

Makes 4 servings

Prep Time: 15 minutes

Bake Time: 30 minutes

1 can (10 ³/₄ ounces) Campbell's® Condensed Cream of Chicken Soup (Regular *or* 98% Fat Free)

¹/₄ cup milk

³/₄ cup shredded Cheddar cheese

¹/₄ teaspoon ground black pepper

1 bag (16 ounces) frozen vegetable combination (broccoli, cauliflower, carrots), thawed

2 cans (4.5 ounces *each*) Swanson® Premium Chunk Chicken Breast in Water, drained

1 package (7.5 ounces) refrigerated biscuits (10 biscuits)

1. Heat the oven to 400°F. Stir the soup, milk, cheese and black pepper in a 3-quart shallow baking dish. Stir in the vegetables and chicken.

2. Bake for 15 minutes or until the chicken mixture is hot and bubbling. Stir the chicken mixture.

3. Top the chicken mixture with the biscuits. Bake for 15 minutes or until the biscuits are golden brown.

Kitchen Tip

Use the downtime while this one-dish meal is in the oven to make a fresh tomato salad: slice some tomatoes and drizzle them with balsamic vinegar and olive oil.

Shopping List

Cream of Chicken Soup

milk

Cheddar cheese

frozen vegetable combination

Chunk Chicken Breast

biscuits

Broccoli & Cheese Casserole

Makes 6 servings

Prep Time: 10 minutes

Bake Time: 30 minutes

1 can (10 3/4 ounces) Campbell's® Condensed Cream of Mushroom Soup (Regular **or** 98% Fat Free)

1/2 cup milk

2 teaspoons yellow mustard

1 bag (16 ounces) frozen broccoli flowerets, thawed

1 cup shredded Cheddar cheese (about 4 ounces)

1/3 cup dry bread crumbs

2 teaspoons butter, melted

1. Stir the soup, milk, mustard, broccoli and cheese in a 1 1/2-quart casserole.

2. Mix the bread crumbs with the butter in a small bowl. Sprinkle the crumb mixture over the broccoli mixture.

3. Bake at 350°F. for 30 minutes or until the mixture is hot and bubbling.

Rice Is Nice: Add **2 cups** cooked white rice to the broccoli mixture before baking.

Cheese Change-Up: Substitute mozzarella cheese for Cheddar.

Shopping List

Cream of Mushroom
Soup

milk

mustard

broccoli

Cheddar cheese

bread crumbs

butter

Chicken Noodle Casserole

Makes 4 servings

Prep Time: 10 minutes

Cook Time: 25 minutes

Shopping List

Cream of Mushroom Soup

milk

butter

broccoli

chicken

egg noodles

Parmesan cheese

1 can (10 3/4 ounces) Campbell's® Condensed Cream of Mushroom Soup (Regular *or* 98% Fat Free)

1/2 cup milk

2 tablespoons butter, melted

1/4 teaspoon ground black pepper

1 cup frozen broccoli flowerets, thawed

2 cups shredded cooked chicken

2 cups hot cooked medium egg noodles

1/2 cup grated Parmesan cheese

1. Stir soup, milk, butter, black pepper, broccoli, chicken and noodles in a 2-quart casserole.

2. Bake at 400°F. for 20 minutes or until hot. Stir.

3. Sprinkle with the cheese. Bake for 5 minutes more.

Sloppy Joe Casserole

Makes 5 servings

Prep Time: 15 minutes

Bake Time: 15 minutes

1 pound ground beef

1 can (10 3/4 ounces) Campbell's® Condensed Tomato Soup (Regular *or* Healthy Request®)

1/4 cup water

1 teaspoon Worcestershire sauce

1/8 teaspoon ground black pepper

1 package (7.5 ounces) refrigerated biscuits (10 biscuits)

1/2 cup shredded Cheddar cheese

1. Heat the oven to 400°F.

2. Cook the beef in a 10-inch skillet over medium-high heat until it's well browned, stirring often to separate meat. Pour off any fat.

3. Stir the soup, water, Worcestershire and black pepper in the skillet and heat to a boil. Spoon the beef mixture into a 1 1/2-quart casserole. Arrange the biscuits around the inside edge of the casserole.

4. Bake for 15 minutes or until the biscuits are golden brown. Sprinkle the cheese over the beef mixture.

Shopping List

ground beef

Tomato Soup

Worcestershire sauce

biscuits

Cheddar cheese

Kitchen Tip

Sharp or mild Cheddar cheese will work in this recipe.

Baked Macaroni & Cheese

Makes 4 servings

Prep Time: 20 minutes

Cook Time: 20 minutes

1 can (10 ¾ ounces) Campbell's® Condensed Cheddar Cheese Soup

½ soup can milk

⅛ teaspoon ground black pepper

1½ cups corkscrew *or* medium shell-shaped pasta, cooked and drained

1 tablespoon dry bread crumbs

2 teaspoons butter, melted

Shopping List

Cheddar Cheese Soup

milk

pasta

bread crumbs

butter

1. Stir the soup, milk, black pepper and pasta in a 1-quart casserole.

2. Mix the bread crumbs with the butter in a small bowl. Sprinkle over the pasta mixture.

3. Bake at 400°F. for 20 minutes or until hot.

To Double Recipe: Double all ingredients, except increase butter to **1 tablespoon**, use 2-quart casserole and increase baking time to 25 minutes.

Variation: Substitute **2 cups** hot cooked elbow macaroni (about 1 cup **uncooked**) for corkscrew or shell-shaped pasta.

Hearty Chicken & Noodle Casserole

Makes 4 servings

Prep Time: 15 minutes

Bake Time: 25 minutes

Shopping List

Cream of Mushroom
Soup

milk

mixed vegetables

chicken

egg noodles

Parmesan cheese

Cheddar cheese

1 can (10 $3/4$ ounces) Campbell's® Condensed Cream of Mushroom Soup (Regular *or* 98% Fat Free)

$1/2$ cup milk

$1/4$ teaspoon ground black pepper

1 cup frozen mixed vegetables

2 cups cubed cooked chicken

$1/4$ of a 12-ounce package medium egg noodles (about 2 cups), cooked and drained

$1/4$ cup grated Parmesan cheese

$1/2$ cup shredded Cheddar cheese

1. Heat the oven to 400°F. Stir the soup, milk, black pepper, vegetables, chicken, noodles and Parmesan cheese in a $1^1/2$-quart casserole.

2. Bake for 25 minutes or until the chicken mixture is hot and bubbling. Stir the chicken mixture. Top with the Cheddar cheese.

Kitchen Tip

Easy casseroles like this one are a simple way to transform leftovers. Cooked chicken, turkey or ham will all work in this recipe.

Beef and Mozzarella Bake

Makes 6 servings

Prep Time: 10 minutes

Cook Time: 35 minutes

1 pound ground beef

1 teaspoon dried basil leaves, crushed

¼ teaspoon ground black pepper

⅛ teaspoon garlic powder *or* 1 clove garlic, minced

1¼ cups Prego® Traditional Italian Sauce

1 can (10¾ ounces) Campbell's® Condensed Cream of Mushroom Soup (Regular *or* 98% Fat Free)

1¼ cups water

1½ cups shredded mozzarella cheese (6 ounces)

3 cups medium shell-shaped pasta, cooked and drained

Shopping List

ground beef

basil

garlic powder

Traditional Italian Sauce

Cream of Mushroom Soup

mozzarella cheese

shell-shaped pasta

1. Cook the beef, basil, black pepper and garlic powder in a 10-inch skillet over medium-high heat until well browned, stirring frequently to separate meat. Pour off any fat.

2. Stir the Italian sauce, soup, water and **1 cup** of the mozzarella cheese into the skillet. Stir in the pasta to coat with the sauce mixture. Spoon into a 2-quart shallow baking dish. Sprinkle with the remaining cheese.

3. Bake at 400°F. for 25 minutes or until hot and bubbling.

Cheesy Chicken & Rice Casserole

Makes 4 servings

Prep Time: 15 minutes

Bake Time: 50 minutes

Stand Time: 10 minutes

1 can (10 3/4 ounces) Campbell's® Condensed Cream of Chicken Soup (Regular *or* 98% Fat Free)

1 1/3 cups water

3/4 cup **uncooked** regular long-grain white rice

1/2 teaspoon onion powder

1/4 teaspoon ground black pepper

2 cups frozen mixed vegetables

4 skinless, boneless chicken breast halves

1/2 cup shredded Cheddar cheese

1. Heat the oven to 375°F. Stir the soup, water, rice, onion powder, black pepper and vegetables in a 2-quart shallow baking dish.

2. Top with the chicken. Season the chicken as desired. Cover the baking dish.

3. Bake for 50 minutes or until the chicken is cooked through and the rice is tender. Top with the cheese. Let the casserole stand for 10 minutes. Stir the rice before serving.

Shopping List

Cream of Chicken Soup

rice

onion powder

mixed vegetables

chicken

Cheddar cheese

Kitchen Tip

To try it Alfredo, substitute broccoli flowerets for the vegetables and substitute 1/4 cup grated Parmesan for the Cheddar cheese. Add 2 tablespoons Parmesan cheese with the soup. Sprinkle the chicken with the remaining Parmesan cheese.

Trim It Down: Use **Campbell's**® 98% Fat Free Condensed Cream of Chicken Soup instead of regular soup and use low-fat cheese instead of regular cheese.

Mexican: In place of onion powder and pepper use **1 teaspoon** chili powder. Substitute Mexican cheese blend for Cheddar.

Italian: In place of onion powder and pepper use **1 teaspoon** Italian seasoning, crushed. Substitute ⅓ **cup** shredded Parmesan for Cheddar.

Garlic Mashed Potatoes & Beef Bake

Makes 4 servings

Prep Time: 15 minutes

Bake Time: 20 minutes

Shopping List

ground beef

Cream of Mushroom with Roasted Garlic Soup

Worcestershire sauce

frozen vegetable combination

butter

milk

mashed potato flakes

1 pound ground beef

1 can (10 3/4 ounces) Campbell's® Condensed Cream of Mushroom with Roasted Garlic Soup

1 tablespoon Worcestershire sauce

1 bag (16 ounces) frozen vegetable combination (broccoli, cauliflower, carrots), thawed

2 cups water

3 tablespoons butter

3/4 cup milk

2 cups instant mashed potato flakes

1. Heat the oven to 400°F. Cook the beef in a 10-inch skillet over medium-high heat until it's well browned, stirring often to separate meat. Pour off any fat.

2. Stir the beef, *1/2 **can*** soup, Worcestershire and vegetables in a 2-quart shallow baking dish.

3. Heat the water, butter and remaining soup in a 3-quart saucepan over medium heat to a boil. Remove the saucepan from the heat. Stir in the milk. Stir in the potatoes. Spoon the potatoes over the beef mixture.

4. Bake for 20 minutes or until the potatoes are lightly browned.

Kitchen Tip

You can use your favorite frozen vegetable combination in this recipe.

Chicken Broccoli Divan

Makes 4 servings

Prep Time: 10 minutes

Bake Time: 20 minutes

Shopping List

broccoli

chicken

Cream of Chicken Soup

milk

Cheddar cheese

bread crumbs

butter

  4 cups cooked broccoli flowerets

$1\frac{1}{2}$ cups cubed cooked chicken

  1 can ($10\frac{3}{4}$ ounces) Campbell's® Condensed Cream of Chicken Soup (Regular *or* 98% Fat Free)

$\frac{1}{3}$ cup milk

$\frac{1}{2}$ cup shredded Cheddar cheese

  2 tablespoons dry bread crumbs

  1 tablespoon butter, melted

1. Heat the oven to 450°F. Place the broccoli and chicken into a 9-inch deep-dish pie plate.

2. Stir the soup and milk in a small bowl. Pour the soup mixture over the broccoli and chicken. Sprinkle with the cheese. Stir the bread crumbs and butter in a small bowl. Sprinkle the bread crumbs over the cheese.

3. Bake for 20 minutes or until the cheese is melted and the bread crumbs are golden brown.

Kitchen Tip

You can use leftover cooked turkey instead of the chicken in this recipe.

Creamy 3-Cheese Pasta

Makes 4 servings

1 can (10¾ ounces) Campbell's® Condensed Cream of Mushroom Soup (Regular *or* 98% Fat Free)

1 cup milk

¼ teaspoon ground black pepper

1 package (8 ounces) shredded two-cheese blend

⅓ cup grated Parmesan cheese

3 cups corkscrew-shaped pasta (rotelle), cooked and drained

Prep Time: 20 minutes

Bake Time: 20 minutes

1. Stir the soup, milk, black pepper and cheeses in a 1½-quart casserole dish. Stir in the pasta.

2. Bake at 400°F. for 20 minutes or until hot.

3. Stir before serving.

Shopping List

Cream of Mushroom Soup

milk

shredded cheese

Parmesan cheese

corkscrew-shaped pasta

Monterey Chicken Tortilla Casserole

Makes 4 servings

Prep Time: 15 minutes

Bake Time: 40 minutes

Shopping List

tortilla chips

chicken

cream-style corn

Picante Sauce

olives

Cheddar cheese

green pepper

1 cup coarsely crumbled tortilla chips

2 cups cubed cooked chicken *or* turkey

1 can (about 15 ounces) cream-style corn

3/4 cup Pace® Picante Sauce

1/2 cup sliced pitted ripe olives

2 ounces shredded Cheddar cheese (about 1/2 cup)

Chopped green *or* red pepper

Tortilla chips

1. Layer the crumbled chips, chicken, corn and picante sauce in a 1-quart casserole. Top with the olives and cheese.

2. Bake at 350°F. for 40 minutes or until the mixture is hot and bubbling. Top with the pepper. Serve with the chips.

Tuna Noodle Casserole

Makes 8 servings

2 cans (10 ³/₄ ounces *each*) Campbell's® Condensed Cream of Mushroom Soup (Regular *or* 98% Fat Free)

1 cup milk

2 cups frozen peas

2 cans (about 10 ounces *each*) tuna, drained

¹/₂ of a 12-ounce package medium egg noodles (about 4 cups), cooked and drained

2 tablespoons dry bread crumbs

1 tablespoon butter, melted

Prep Time: 10 minutes

Bake Time: 35 minutes

Shopping List

Cream of Mushroom Soup

milk

peas

tuna

egg noodles

bread crumbs

butter

1. Stir the soup, milk, peas, tuna and noodles in a 3-quart casserole.

2. Bake at 400°F. for 30 minutes or until the tuna mixture is hot and bubbling. Stir the tuna mixture.

3. Stir the bread crumbs and butter in a small bowl. Sprinkle the bread crumb mixture over the tuna mixture. Bake for 5 minutes or until the topping is golden brown.

Do-Ahead
Dishes

Make it now, serve it later—

a little planning is all it takes

Corn and Black-Eyed Pea Salad

Makes 8 servings

Prep Time: 15 minutes

Chill Time: 4 hours

Shopping List

corn

black-eyed peas

green pepper

onion

cilantro

Chunky Salsa

1 bag (16 ounces) frozen whole kernel corn, thawed (about 3 cups)

1 can (about 15 ounces) black-eyed peas, rinsed and drained

1 large green pepper, chopped (about 1 cup)

1 medium onion, chopped (about 1/2 cup)

1/2 cup chopped fresh cilantro leaves

1 jar (16 ounces) Pace® Chunky Salsa

1. Place the corn, peas, green pepper, onion and cilantro into a medium bowl. Add the salsa and stir to coat.

2. Cover and refrigerate for 4 hours. Stir before serving.

Kitchen Tip

To make ahead, prepare salad as directed. Cover and refrigerate overnight. Stir before serving.

Three Cheese Baked Ziti with Spinach

Makes 6 servings

Prep Time: 15 minutes

Bake Time: 30 minutes

1 box (16 ounces) medium tube-shaped pasta (ziti)

1 bag (6 ounces) baby spinach leaves (4 cups), washed

1 jar (1 pound 9 ounces) Prego® Marinara Italian Sauce

1 cup ricotta cheese

1 cup shredded mozzarella cheese (4 ounces)

³/₄ cup grated Parmesan cheese

¹/₂ teaspoon garlic powder

¹/₄ teaspoon ground black pepper

Shopping List

ziti

spinach

Marinara Italian Sauce

ricotta cheese

mozzarella cheese

Parmesan cheese

garlic powder

1. Prepare the pasta according to the package directions. Add the spinach during the last minute of the cooking time. Drain the pasta and spinach well in a colander. Return them to the saucepot.

2. Stir the Italian sauce, ricotta, ¹/₂ **cup** of the mozzarella cheese, ¹/₂ **cup** of the Parmesan cheese, garlic powder and black pepper into the pasta mixture. Spoon the pasta mixture into a 13×9×2-inch shallow baking dish. Sprinkle with the remaining mozzarella and Parmesan cheeses.

3. Bake at 350°F. for 30 minutes or until hot and bubbling.

Kitchen Tip

Prepare through step 2. Cover and refrigerate up to 6 hours. Uncover and let come to room temperature before baking.

Eggplant Tomato Gratin

Makes 8 servings

Prep Time: 20 minutes

Bake Time: 25 minutes

Stand Time: 10 minutes

Shopping List

eggplant

Cream of Celery Soup

milk

Parmesan cheese

tomatoes

onion

basil

bread crumbs

olive oil

Vegetable cooking spray

1 large eggplant (about 1¼ pounds) cut into
½-inch-thick slices

1 can (10¾ ounces) Campbell's® Condensed Cream
of Celery Soup (Regular *or* 98% Fat Free)

½ cup milk

¼ cup grated Parmesan cheese

2 large tomatoes, cut into ½-inch-thick slices
(about 2 cups)

1 medium onion, thinly sliced (about ½ cup)

¼ cup chopped fresh basil leaves

¼ cup Italian-seasoned dry bread crumbs

1 tablespoon chopped fresh parsley (optional)

1 tablespoon olive oil

1. Heat the oven to 425°F. Spray a baking sheet with cooking spray. Arrange the eggplant in a single layer. Bake for 20 minutes or until tender, turning halfway through baking. Spray 3-quart shallow baking dish with cooking spray.

2. Stir the soup, milk and cheese in a small bowl.

3. Layer **half** the eggplant, tomatoes, onion, basil and soup mixture in the prepared dish. Repeat the layers.

4. Stir the bread crumbs, parsley and oil in a small bowl. Sprinkle over the soup mixture.

5. Reduce the heat to 400°F. and bake for 25 minutes or until hot and golden brown. Let stand for 10 minutes.

Kitchen Tip

*Prepare ahead up to topping with the bread crumb
mixture. Cover and refrigerate overnight. Add
the bread crumb mixture and bake at 400°F. for
30 minutes or until hot and golden brown.*

Chipotle Pork Taco Cups

Makes 10 servings

Prep Time: 15 minutes

Bake Time: 5 minutes

Cook Time: 5 minutes

Vegetable cooking spray

10 whole wheat **or** flour tortillas (6-inch)

1 container (18 ounces) refrigerated cooked barbecue sauce with shredded pork (about 2 cups)

1 cup Pace® Chunky Salsa

¼ teaspoon ground chipotle chile pepper

Shredded Cheddar cheese (optional)

Guacamole (optional)

Sour cream (optional)

Sliced ripe olives (optional)

Shopping List

tortillas

barbecue sauce with pork

Chunky Salsa

chipotle chile pepper

1. Heat the oven to 350°F. Spray **10** (3-inch) muffin-pan cups with the cooking spray.

2. Wrap the tortillas between damp paper towels. Microwave on HIGH for 30 seconds or until the tortillas are warm. Fold **1** tortilla into thirds to form a cone shape. Press the tortilla cone, wide end down, into a muffin-pan cup. Repeat with the remaining tortillas, rewarming in the microwave as needed.

3. Bake for 5 minutes or until the tortilla cones are golden. Remove the tortillas from the pan and cool on wire racks.

4. Heat the pork, salsa and chipotle chile pepper in a 2-quart saucepan over medium heat until the mixture is hot and bubbling, stirring often.

5. Spoon about ¼ **cup** pork mixture into **each** tortilla cone. Top with the cheese, guacamole, sour cream or olives, if desired.

Kitchen Tip

You can prepare the tortillas through step 3 up to 24 hours ahead of time and store them in an airtight container.

Japanese Beef Stir-Fry

Makes 8 servings

Prep Time: 30 minutes

Cook Time: 20 minutes

3 tablespoons cornstarch

1 can (10½ ounces) Campbell's® Condensed Beef Broth

½ cup soy sauce

2 tablespoons sugar

2 tablespoons vegetable oil

2 pounds boneless beef sirloin **or** top round steak (¾-inch thick), cut into strips

4 cups sliced shiitake mushrooms (about 7 ounces)

1 head Chinese cabbage (bok choy), thinly sliced (about 6 cups)

2 medium red peppers, cut into 2-inch-long strips (about 3 cups)

3 stalks celery, sliced (about 1½ cups)

2 medium green onions, cut into 2-inch pieces (about ½ cup)

Hot cooked rice

1. Stir the cornstarch, broth, soy sauce and sugar in a small cup. Set the mixture aside.

2. Heat **1 tablespoon** of the oil in a 4-quart saucepan or wok over high heat. Add the beef in 2 batches and stir-fry until it's browned. Remove the beef with a slotted spoon and set it aside.

3. Reduce the heat to medium and add the remaining oil. Add the mushrooms, cabbage, peppers, celery and green onions in 2 batches. Stir-fry until the vegetables are tender-crisp. Remove the vegetables with a slotted spoon and set them aside.

4. Stir the cornstarch mixture and stir it into the saucepan. Cook and stir until the mixture boils and thickens. Return the beef and vegetables to the saucepan and cook until the mixture is hot and bubbling. Serve over rice.

Kitchen Tips

To make slicing beef easier, freeze beef for 1 hour.

Prepare vegetables and place in resealable plastic bags. Refrigerate overnight.

Ham and Broccoli Swirls

Makes 32 appetizers

Thaw Time: 30 minutes

Prep Time: 20 minutes

Cook Time: 15 minutes

½ of a 17¼-ounce package Pepperidge Farm® Frozen Puff Pastry Sheets (1 sheet)

1 egg

1 tablespoon water

1 container (4 ounces) whipped cream cheese with chives spread

1 package (10 ounces) frozen chopped broccoli (2 cups), thawed and well drained

1 cup finely chopped cooked ham

Shopping List

Puff Pastry

egg

cream cheese
with chives

broccoli

ham

1. Thaw pastry sheet at room temperature 30 minutes. Preheat oven to 400°F. Mix egg and water and set aside.

2. Unfold pastry on lightly floured surface. Roll into 16×12-inch rectangle. Spread cream cheese over rectangle to within ½ inch of edges. Top with broccoli and ham. Starting at long side, roll up like a jelly roll, only to center. Roll up opposite side to center. Brush between rolls with egg mixture, then gently press rolls together.

3. Cut into **32** (½-inch) slices. Place 2 inches apart on greased baking sheet. Brush tops with egg mixture.

4. Bake 15 minutes or until golden. Serve warm or at room temperature.

Kitchen Tip

To make ahead, prepare through step 3. Freeze. When frozen, store in plastic bag up to 1 month. To bake, preheat oven to 400°F. Place frozen slices on baking sheet. Bake 20 minutes or until golden.

Ginger Peach Barbecued Chicken

Makes 8 servings

Prep Time: 5 minutes

Cook Time: 40 minutes

2 tablespoons cornstarch

1 can (10½ ounces) Campbell's® Condensed Chicken Broth

½ cup peach preserves

2 tablespoons dry sherry

1 tablespoon soy sauce

½ teaspoon ground ginger

4½ pounds chicken parts

Shopping List

cornstarch

Chicken Broth

peach preserves

sherry

soy sauce

ginger

chicken

1. Stir the cornstarch, broth, preserves, sherry, soy sauce and ginger in a 2-quart saucepan. Cook and stir over medium-high heat until the mixture boils and thickens. Remove the saucepan from the heat. Use **1 cup** broth mixture for basting.

2. Lightly oil the grill rack and heat the grill to medium. Grill the chicken for 20 minutes, turning the chicken over once during grilling. Grill for 20 minutes more or until the chicken is cooked through, turning and brushing often with the reserved broth mixture. Discard the reserved broth mixture.

3. Serve the chicken with the remaining broth mixture.

Kitchen Tip

The broth mixture can be made ahead up to 24 hours. Cover and refrigerate until ready to use.

Now & Later Baked Ziti

Makes 12 servings

Prep Time: 15 minutes

Cook Time: 30 minutes

Shopping List

ground beef

onion

Fresh Mushroom
Italian Sauce

ziti

mozzarella cheese

Parmesan cheese

2 pounds ground beef

1 large onion, chopped (about 1 cup)

7 ½ cups Prego® Fresh Mushroom Italian Sauce

1 package (1 pound) medium tube-shaped pasta (ziti *or* penne) (about 6 cups), cooked and drained

3 cups shredded mozzarella cheese (about 12 ounces)

½ cup grated *or* shredded Parmesan cheese

1. Cook the beef and onion in an 8-quart saucepot over medium high heat until the beef is well browned, stirring often to separate meat. Pour off any fat.

2. Stir the sauce, ziti and *2 cups* mozzarella cheese in the saucepot. Spoon the beef mixture into *2* (12 ½ × 8 ½ × 2-inch) disposable foil pans. Top with the remaining mozzarella and Parmesan cheeses.

3. Bake at 350°F. for 30 minutes or until the beef mixture is hot and the cheese is melted.

Kitchen Tip

To make ahead and freeze, prepare the ziti as directed above but do not bake. Cover the pans with foil and freeze. Bake the frozen ziti, uncovered, at 350°F. for 1 hour or until it's hot. Or, thaw the ziti in the refrigerator for 24 hours, then bake, uncovered, at 350°F. for 45 minutes or until it's hot.

Bulgur Salad

Makes 6 servings

1¼ cups water

1 cup **uncooked** bulgur wheat

1 cup Pace® Pico De Gallo **or** Pace® Picante Sauce

1 cup rinsed, drained canned black beans

1 cup drained canned whole kernel corn

¼ cup chopped fresh cilantro leaves

Prep Time: 10 minutes

Cook Time: 5 minutes

Stand Time: 20 minutes

1. Heat the water in a 2-quart saucepan over medium-high heat to a boil. Stir the bulgur into the saucepan. Remove the saucepan from the heat. Let stand for 20 minutes.

2. Stir the bulgur, pico de gallo, beans, corn and cilantro in a medium bowl. Serve immediately or cover and refrigerate until ready to serve.

Kitchen Tip

For a twist, stir in a squeeze of fresh lime juice.

Shopping List

bulgur

Pico De Gallo

black beans

corn

cilantro

Spinach and Mushroom Frittata

Makes 8 servings

Prep Time: 10 minutes

Bake Time: 35 minutes

Vegetable cooking spray

10 eggs

1 can (10 3/4 ounces) Campbell's® Condensed Cream of Mushroom Soup (Regular *or* 98% Fat Free)

1 package (10 ounces) frozen chopped spinach, thawed and well drained

1 1/2 cups shredded Swiss cheese *or* Jarlsberg cheese (about 6 ounces)

1/2 teaspoon ground black pepper

1. Heat the oven to 375°F. Spray a 2-quart shallow baking dish with the cooking spray.

2. Beat the eggs in a large bowl with a fork or whisk. Stir in the soup. Stir in the spinach, **1 cup** of the cheese and black pepper. Pour the egg mixture into the baking dish.

3. Bake for 35 minutes or until the eggs are set. Sprinkle with the remaining cheese.

Shopping List

eggs

Cream of Mushroom Soup

spinach

Swiss cheese

Kitchen Tip

You can prepare the frittata as directed above then cover and refrigerate for up to 24 hours. Before serving, remove the frittata from the refrigerator and let stand for about 30 minutes. Heat the oven to 350°F. Bake for 20 minutes or until hot.

Simple
Slow Cooking

A quick prep in the morning

and dinner's ready at night

Chipotle Chili

Makes 8 servings

Prep Time: 15 minutes

Cook Time: 8 hours

Shopping List

Chunky Salsa

chili powder

chipotle chile pepper

onion

beef for stew

kidney beans

1 jar (16 ounces) Pace® Chunky Salsa

1 cup water

2 tablespoons chili powder

1 teaspoon ground chipotle chile pepper

1 large onion, chopped (about 1 cup)

2 pounds beef for stew, cut into 1/2-inch pieces

1 can (about 19 ounces) red kidney beans, rinsed
   and drained

   Shredded Cheddar cheese (optional)

   Sour cream (optional)

1. Stir the salsa, water, chili powder, chipotle pepper, onion, beef and beans in a 3½-quart slow cooker.

2. Cover and cook on LOW for 8 to 9 hours* or until the beef is fork-tender. Serve with the cheese and sour cream, if desired.

Or on HIGH for 4 to 5 hours.

Golden Chicken with Noodles

Makes 8 servings

Prep Time: **5 minutes**

Cook Time: **7 hours**

Shopping List

Cream of Chicken
Soup

lemon juice

Dijon mustard

garlic powder

carrots

chicken

egg noodles

parsley

2 cans (10 3/4 ounces *each*) Campbell's® Condensed
   Cream of Chicken Soup (Regular *or*
   98% Fat Free)

1/2 cup water

1/4 cup lemon juice

1 tablespoon Dijon-style mustard

1 1/2 teaspoons garlic powder

8 large carrots, thickly sliced (about 6 cups)

8 skinless, boneless chicken breast halves

1/2 of a 12-ounce package egg noodles
   (about 4 cups), cooked and drained

   Chopped fresh parsley

1. Stir the soup, water, lemon juice, mustard, garlic
powder and carrots in a 3 1/2-quart slow cooker. Add the
chicken and turn to coat.

2. Cover and cook on LOW for 7 to 8 hours* or until
the chicken is cooked through. Serve with the noodles.
Sprinkle with the parsley.

Or on HIGH for 4 to 5 hours.

Turkey Fajita Wraps

Makes 8 servings

Prep Time: *10 minutes*

Cook Time: *6 hours*

Shopping List

Chunky Salsa

green or red peppers

corn

chili powder

lime juice

garlic

turket breast cutlets

tortillas

Mexican cheese
blend

2 cups Pace® Chunky Salsa

2 large green *or* red peppers, cut into 2-inch-long strips (about 4 cups)

1½ cups frozen whole kernel corn, thawed

1 tablespoon chili powder

2 tablespoons lime juice

3 cloves garlic, minced

2 pounds turkey breast cutlets, cut into 4-inch-long strips

16 flour tortillas (8-inch), warmed

Shredded Mexican cheese blend

1. Stir the salsa, peppers, corn, chili powder, lime juice, garlic and turkey in a 4-quart slow cooker.

2. Cover and cook on LOW for 6 to 7 hours* or until the turkey is cooked through.

3. Spoon *about ½ cup* of the turkey mixture down the center of *each* tortilla. Top with the cheese. Fold the tortillas around the filling.

*Or on HIGH for 3 to 4 hours.

Bacon Potato Chowder

Makes 8 servings

4 slices bacon, cooked and crumbled

1 large onion, chopped (about 1 cup)

4 cans (10 3/4 ounces *each*) Campbell's® Condensed
   Cream of Potato Soup

4 soup cans milk

1/4 teaspoon ground black pepper

2 large russet potatoes, cut into 1/2-inch pieces
   (about 3 cups)

1/2 cup chopped fresh chives

2 cups shredded Cheddar cheese (8 ounces)

Prep Time: 15 minutes

Cook Time: 3 hours

Shopping List

bacon

onion

Cream of Potato Soup

milk

potatoes

chives

Cheddar cheese

1. Stir the bacon, onion, soup, milk, black pepper, potatoes and **1/4 cup** chives in a 6-quart slow cooker.

2. Cover and cook on HIGH for 3 to 4 hours or until the potatoes are tender.

3. Add the cheese and stir until the cheese is melted. Serve with the remaining chives.

Slow-Cooked Taco Shredded Beef

Makes 16 tacos

Prep Time: 10 minutes

Cook Time: 6 hours

Stand Time: 10 minutes

Shopping List

French Onion Soup

chili powder

cumin

beef roast

cilantro

taco shells

Cheddar cheese

lettuce

sour cream

1 can ($10^3/_4$ ounces) Campbell's® Condensed French Onion Soup

1 tablespoon chili powder

$^1/_2$ teaspoon ground cumin

2-pound boneless beef chuck roast

2 tablespoons finely chopped fresh cilantro leaves

16 taco shells

1 cup shredded Cheddar cheese (about 4 ounces)

Shredded lettuce

Sour cream

1. Stir the soup, chili powder and cumin in a 4-quart slow cooker. Add the beef and turn to coat.

2. Cover and cook on LOW for 6 to 7 hours* or until the beef is fork-tender.

3. Remove the beef from the cooker to a cutting board and let stand for 10 minutes. Using 2 forks, shred the beef. Return the beef to the cooker. Stir the cilantro in the cooker.

4. Spoon **about $^1/_4$ cup** beef mixture into **each** taco shell. Top **each** with **about 1 tablespoon** cheese. Top with the lettuce and the sour cream.

Or on HIGH for 4 to 5 hours.

Not Your Gramma's Kugel

Makes 6 servings

Prep Time: 10 minutes

Cook Time: 2 hours

Shopping List

egg noodles

currants

Cheddar Cheese Soup

cottage cheese

sugar

orange

eggs

Vegetable cooking spray

1 package (12 ounces) **uncooked** medium egg noodles (about 7 cups)

½ cup currants

1 can (10¾ ounces) Campbell's® Condensed Cheddar Cheese Soup

1 cup cottage cheese

¾ cup sugar

1 teaspoon grated orange zest

2 eggs

1. Spray the inside of a 3½-quart slow cooker with the cooking spray.

2. Cook the noodles according to the package directions until almost done. Drain and place in the cooker. Sprinkle with the currants.

3. Beat the soup, cottage cheese, sugar, orange zest and eggs in a medium bowl with a fork. Pour over the noodles. Stir to coat.

4. Cover and cook on LOW for 2 to 2½ hours or until set. Serve warm.

Kitchen Tip

This versatile sweet noodle pudding can be served as a dessert, a brunch dish, or a side dish alongside barbecued chicken or brisket.

Coq au Vin

Makes 6 servings

Prep Time: 10 minutes

Cook Time: 8 hours

Shopping List

mushrooms

frozen onions

rosemary

chicken

cornstarch

Golden Mushroom Soup

dry red wine

potatoes

1 package (10 ounces) sliced mushrooms

1 bag (16 ounces) frozen whole small white onions

1 sprig fresh rosemary leaves

2 pounds skinless, boneless chicken thighs *and/or* breasts, cut into 1-inch strips

¼ cup cornstarch

1 can (10¾ ounces) Campbell's® Condensed Golden Mushroom Soup

1 cup Burgundy *or* other dry red wine

Hot mashed *or* oven-roasted potatoes

1. Place the mushrooms, onions, rosemary and chicken into a 3½-quart slow cooker.

2. Stir the cornstarch, soup and wine in a small bowl. Pour over the chicken and vegetables.

3. Cover and cook on LOW for 8 to 9 hours*. Remove the rosemary. Serve with the mashed potatoes.

*Or on HIGH for 4 to 5 hours.

Savory Pot Roast

Makes 6 servings

1 can (10 ³/₄ ounces) Campbell's® Condensed Cream
   of Mushroom Soup (Regular *or* 98% Fat Free)

1 pouch (1 ounce) dry onion soup & recipe mix

6 small red potatoes, cut in half

6 medium carrots, cut into 2-inch pieces (about
   3 cups)

   3- to 3¹/₂-pound boneless beef bottom round
   roast *or* chuck pot roast

1. Stir the soup, onion soup mix, potatoes and carrots in
a 4¹/₂-quart slow cooker. Add the beef and turn to coat.

2. Cover and cook on LOW for 8 to 9 hours* or until
the beef is fork-tender.

Or on HIGH for 4 to 5 hours.

Prep Time: 10 minutes

Cook Time: 8 hours

Shopping List

Cream of Mushroom
Soup

dry onion soup mix

red potatoes

carrots

beef roast

Creamy Blush Sauce with Turkey and Penne

Makes 8 servings

Prep Time: 10 minutes

Cook Time: 7 hours

4   turkey thighs, skin removed (about 3 pounds)

1   jar (1 pound 9.75 ounces) Prego® Chunky Garden Mushroom & Green Pepper Italian Sauce

¹/₂ teaspoon crushed red pepper

¹/₂ cup half-and-half

     Hot cooked tube-shaped pasta (penne)

     Grated Parmesan cheese

Shopping List

turkey thighs

Chunky Garden Mushroom & Green Pepper Italian Sauce

crushed red pepper

half-and-half

penne pasta

Parmesan cheese

1. Put the turkey in a 3¹/₂- to 5-quart slow cooker. Pour the Italian sauce over the turkey and sprinkle with the red pepper.

2. Cover and cook on LOW for 7 to 8 hours* or until turkey is fork-tender and cooked through. Remove the turkey from the cooker. Remove the turkey meat from the bones and cut it into cubes.

3. Stir the turkey meat and the half-and-half into the cooker. Cover and cook for 10 minutes or until hot. Spoon the sauce over the turkey and pasta. Sprinkle with cheese.

*Or on HIGH for 4 to 5 hours.

Kitchen Tip

Substitute 8 bone-in chicken thighs (about 2 pounds) for the turkey thighs. Serves 4.

Chicken & Bean Burritos

Makes 12 burritos

Prep Time: 10 minutes

Cook Time: 6 hours

Shopping List

Cheddar Cheese Soup

garlic powder

chili powder

chicken thighs

black beans

pinto beans

tortillas

lettuce

tomato

1 can (10 3/4 ounces) Campbell's® Condensed Cheddar Cheese Soup

1 teaspoon garlic powder

2 tablespoons chili powder

2 pounds skinless, boneless chicken thighs, cut into 1-inch pieces

1 can (about 14 ounces) black beans, rinsed and drained

1 can (about 14 ounces) pinto beans, rinsed and drained

12 flour tortillas (8- to 10-inch), warmed

Chopped lettuce

Chopped tomato

1. Stir the soup, garlic powder, chili powder and chicken in a 3 1/2- to 4-quart slow cooker.

2. Cover and cook on LOW for 6 to 7 hours* or until the chicken is cooked through.

3. Mash the black and pinto beans with a fork in a medium bowl. Stir into the chicken mixture. Spoon *about 1/2 cup* of the chicken mixture down the center of *each* tortilla. Top with the lettuce and tomato. Fold the tortillas around the filling.

*Or on HIGH for 3 to 4 hours.

Melt-in-Your-Mouth Short Ribs

Makes 6 servings

Prep Time: 10 minutes

Cook Time: 8 hours

Shopping List

beef short ribs

brown sugar

garlic

thyme

flour

French Onion Soup

dark ale or beer

mashed potatoes

6 serving-sized pieces beef short ribs
   (about 3 pounds)

2 tablespoons packed brown sugar

3 cloves garlic, minced

1 teaspoon dried thyme leaves, crushed

¼ cup all-purpose flour

1 can (10½ ounces) Campbell's® Condensed
   French Onion Soup

1 bottle (12 fluid ounces) dark ale *or* beer

   Hot mashed potatoes *or* egg noodles

1. Place the beef into a 5-quart slow cooker. Add the brown sugar, garlic, thyme and flour and toss to coat.

2. Stir the soup and ale in a small bowl. Pour over the beef.

3. Cover and cook on LOW for 8 to 9 hours* or until the beef is fork-tender. Serve with the mashed potatoes.

Or on HIGH for 4 to 5 hours.

Balsamic Beef with Mushrooms

Makes 6 servings

Vegetable cooking spray

2 pounds boneless beef chuck roast, 1-inch thick

2⅔ cups Prego® Traditional Italian Sauce

⅓ cup balsamic vinegar

2 packages (8 ounces *each*) sliced mushrooms

1 slice bacon, cooked and crumbled

Hot cooked egg noodles

Prep Time: 15 minutes

Cook Time: 7 hours

1. Spray a 10-inch skillet with the cooking spray and heat over medium-high heat for 1 minute. Add the beef and cook until it's well browned on both sides.

2. Stir the Italian sauce, vinegar, mushrooms and bacon in a 5-quart slow cooker. Add the beef and turn to coat.

3. Cover and cook on LOW for 7 to 8 hours* or until the beef is fork-tender. Serve with the egg noodles.

Or on HIGH for 4 to 5 hours.

Shopping List

chuck roast

Traditional Italian Sauce

balsamic vinegar

mushrooms

bacon

egg noodles

Orange Chicken with Green Onions and Walnuts

Makes 4 servings

Prep Time: *10 minutes*

Cook Time: *8 hours*

Shopping List

Chicken Stock

teriyaki sauce

garlic

orange marmalade

green onions

cornstarch

chicken thighs

walnuts

rice

1½ cups Swanson® Chicken Stock

¼ cup teriyaki sauce

3 cloves garlic, minced

¾ cup orange marmalade

4 green onions, sliced (about ½ cup)

2 tablespoons cornstarch

8 chicken thighs, skin removed (about 2 pounds)

½ cup walnut pieces

Hot cooked rice

1. Stir the stock, teriyaki sauce, garlic, marmalade, **¼ cup** green onions and cornstarch in a 6-quart slow cooker. Add the chicken and turn to coat.

2. Cover and cook on LOW for 8 to 9 hours* or until the chicken is cooked through. Sprinkle with the walnuts and remaining green onions. Serve with the rice.

*Or on HIGH for 4 to 5 hours.

Simplified *Sides*

Complement your meal with a

simple and tasty side

Savory Spinach with Blue Cheese and Walnuts

Makes 6 servings

*Prep Time: **15 minutes***

*Cook Time: **15 minutes***

Shopping List

butter

onion

garlic

tomatoes

Chicken Broth

spinach

blue cheese

walnuts

1 tablespoon butter

1 large sweet onion, halved and thinly sliced (about 1 cup)

2 cloves garlic, sliced

2 large tomatoes, seeded and chopped (about 3 cups)

³/₄ cup Swanson® Chicken Broth (Regular, Natural Goodness® *or* Certified Organic)

1 bag (11 ounces) fresh baby spinach

Ground black pepper

¹/₄ cup crumbled blue cheese (about 2 ounces)

2 tablespoons chopped walnuts

1. Melt the butter in a 12-inch nonstick skillet. Add the onion and garlic and cook until they're tender, stirring occasionally.

2. Add the tomatoes, broth and spinach. Cook for 2 minutes or until the spinach wilts. Season with the black pepper. Sprinkle with the cheese and walnuts, if desired.

Cheesy Chile Corn Casserole

Makes 6 servings

Prep Time: 15 minutes

Bake Time: 30 minutes

1 can (10 ¾ ounces) Campbell's® Condensed Cheddar Cheese Soup

¼ cup milk

1 tablespoon butter, melted

Dash ground red pepper

1 bag (16 ounces) frozen whole kernel corn, thawed

1 can (about 4 ounces) chopped green chiles

1 can (2.8 ounces) French fried onions (about 1 ⅓ cups)

Shopping List

Cheddar Cheese Soup

milk

butter

corn

chiles

French fried onions

1. Heat the oven to 350°F. Stir the soup, milk, butter, pepper, corn, chiles and **⅔ cup** onions in a 1½-quart casserole.

2. Bake for 25 minutes or until the corn mixture is hot and bubbling. Stir the corn mixture.

3. Sprinkle the remaining onions over the corn mixture. Bake for 5 minutes or until the onions are golden brown.

Kitchen Tip

An oven thermometer is the best way to check how accurately your oven heats. Most are designed to hang on the rack inside your oven to conveniently measure the oven temperature.

Moist & Savory Stuffing

Makes 11 servings

Prep Time: 20 minutes

Cook Time: 30 minutes

2½ cups Swanson® Chicken Broth (Regular, Natural Goodness® *or* Certified Organic)

2 stalks celery, coarsely chopped (about 1 cup)

1 large onion, coarsely chopped (about 1 cup)

1 package (16 ounces) Pepperidge Farm® Herb Seasoned Stuffing

Shopping List

Chicken Broth

celery

onion

Herb Seasoned Stuffing

1. Heat the broth, celery and onion in a 3-quart saucepan over medium-high heat to a boil. Reduce the heat to low. Cover and cook for 5 minutes or until the vegetables are tender. Add the stuffing and mix lightly.

2. Spoon the stuffing mixture into a greased 3-quart casserole dish. Cover and bake at 350°F. for 30 minutes or until hot.

Kitchen Tip

For a crunchier stuffing, bake the casserole uncovered.

Ultra Creamy Mashed Potatoes

Makes 6 servings

3½ cups Swanson® Chicken Broth (Regular, Natural
   Goodness® *or* Certified Organic)

5 large potatoes, cut into 1-inch pieces
   (about 7½ cups)

½ cup light cream

2 tablespoons butter

   Generous dash ground black pepper

Prep Time: 15 minutes

Cook Time: 20 minutes

1. Heat the broth and potatoes in a 3-quart saucepan over medium-high heat to a boil.

2. Reduce the heat to medium. Cover and cook for 10 minutes or until the potatoes are tender. Drain, reserving the broth.

3. Mash the potatoes with ¼ **cup** broth, cream, butter and black pepper. Add additional broth, if needed, until desired consistency.

Ultimate Mashed Potatoes: Stir ½ **cup** sour cream, **3** slices bacon, cooked and crumbled (reserve some for garnish) and ¼ **cup** chopped fresh chives into the hot mashed potatoes. Sprinkle with the reserved bacon.

Shopping List

Chicken Broth

potatoes

light cream

butter

Cheddar Potato Bake

Makes 8 servings

Prep Time: 10 minutes

Bake Time: 30 minutes

Shopping List

butter

milk

instant potato flakes

Cheddar Cheese Soup

sour cream

green onion

2 cups water

3 tablespoons butter

$^3/_4$ cup milk

2 cups instant potato flakes **or** buds

1 can (10$^3/_4$ ounces) Campbell's® Condensed Cheddar Cheese Soup

$^1/_3$ cup sour cream **or** plain yogurt

   Generous dash ground black pepper

1 medium green onion, chopped (about 2 tablespoons)

1. Heat the water and butter in a 2-quart saucepan over high heat to a boil. Remove from the heat. Stir in the milk. Slowly stir in the potatoes.

2. Stir the potatoes, soup, sour cream, black pepper and green onion in a 1$^1/_2$-quart casserole.

3. Bake at 350°F. for 30 minutes or until hot.

Kitchen Tip

*Substitute **Campbell's**® Condensed Cream of Mushroom Soup for the Cheddar Cheese Soup and chopped roasted sweet peppers for the green onion.*

Picante Pinto Beans with Bacon

Makes 6 servings

Prep Time: *10 minutes*

Cook Time: *5 minutes*

Shopping List

Picante Sauce

ketchup

brown sugar

cumin

bacon

pinto beans

jalapeño pepper

1 cup Pace® Picante Sauce

$1/4$ cup ketchup **or** barbecue sauce

$1/4$ cup packed brown sugar

1 teaspoon ground cumin

4 slices bacon, cooked and crumbled

2 cans (about 15 ounces **each**) pinto beans, rinsed and drained

Sliced jalapeño pepper

Heat the picante sauce, ketchup, brown sugar, cumin, bacon and beans in a 2-quart saucepan over medium heat until the mixture is hot and bubbling. Garnish with the jalapeño pepper.

Kitchen Tip

Try topping these beans with finely shredded Cheddar cheese before serving.

Broth Simmered Rice

Makes 4 servings

1³/₄ cups Swanson® Chicken Broth (Regular, Natural Goodness® *or* Certified Organic)

³/₄ cup *uncooked* regular long-grain white rice

Fresh thyme

Prep Time: 5 minutes

Cook Time: 25 minutes

1. Heat the broth in a 2-quart saucepan over medium-high heat to a boil.

2. Stir in the rice. Reduce the heat to low. Cover and cook for 20 minutes or until the rice is tender and most of the liquid is absorbed. Serve with fresh thyme.

Florentine Simmered Rice: Add *1 teaspoon* dried Italian seasoning to broth. Add *1 cup* chopped spinach with rice. Stir in ¹/₂ *cup* grated Parmesan cheese before serving. Serve with additional cheese.

Shopping List

Chicken Broth

rice

thyme

Kitchen Tip

*This recipe will work with any variety of **Swanson**® Broth.*

Bandito Baked Beans

Makes 6 servings

Prep Time: 5 minutes

Cook Time: 15 minutes

Shopping List

oil

onion

Picante Sauce

molasses

spicy mustard

pork and beans

black beans

1 tablespoon vegetable oil

½ cup chopped onion

1 cup Pace® Picante Sauce

¼ cup molasses

1 tablespoon spicy-brown mustard

1 can (about 15 ounces) pork and beans

1 can (about 15 ounces) black beans, rinsed and drained

1. Heat the oil in a 2-quart saucepan over medium heat. Add the onion and cook until it's tender.

2. Stir the picante sauce, molasses, mustard, pork and beans and black beans in the saucepan and heat to a boil. Reduce the heat to low. Cook for 5 minutes or until the mixture is hot and bubbling.

Green Bean Casserole

Makes 12 servings

2 cans (10 ³/₄ ounces *each*) Campbell's® Condensed Cream of Mushroom Soup (Regular *or* 98% Fat Free)

1 cup milk

2 teaspoons soy sauce

¹/₄ teaspoon ground black pepper

2 bags (about 16 ounces *each*) frozen cut green beans, cooked and drained

1 can (6 ounces) French fried onions (2 ²/₃ cups)

Prep Time: 10 minutes

Cook Time: 30 minutes

Shopping List

Cream of Mushroom Soup

milk

soy sauce

green beans

French fried onions

1. Stir the soup, milk, soy sauce, black pepper, beans and *1 ¹/₃ cups* onions in a 3-quart casserole.

2. Bake at 350°F. for 25 minutes or until the bean mixture is hot and bubbling. Stir the bean mixture and top with the remaining onions.

3. Bake for 5 minutes or until the onions are golden brown.

Creamy Baked Carrots

Makes 6 servings

Prep Time: 5 minutes

Bake Time: 40 minutes

Shopping List

Cream of Celery Soup

milk

thyme

crinkle-cut carrots

French fried onions

Vegetable cooking spray

1 can (10¾ ounces) Campbell's® Condensed Cream of Celery Soup (Regular *or* 98% Fat Free)

½ cup milk

½ teaspoon dried thyme leaves, crushed

1 bag (20 ounces) frozen crinkle-cut carrots, thawed (about 5 cups)

1 can (2.8 ounces) French fried onions (1⅓ cups)

1. Spray a 2-quart casserole with cooking spray. Stir the soup, milk, thyme, carrots and ⅔ **cup** of the onions in the prepared dish.

2. Bake at 350°F. for 35 minutes. Stir the carrot mixture.

3. Sprinkle the remaining onions over the carrot mixture. Bake for 5 minutes more or until carrots are tender and onions are golden brown.

Heavenly Sweet Potatoes

Makes 8 servings

Prep Time: 10 minutes

Bake Time: 20 minutes

Shopping List

sweet potatoes

cinnamon

ginger

Chicken Broth

marshmallows

Vegetable cooking spray

1 can (40 ounces) cut sweet potatoes in heavy syrup, drained

$1/4$ teaspoon ground cinnamon

$1/8$ teaspoon ground ginger

$3/4$ cup Swanson® Chicken Broth (Regular, Natural Goodness® *or* Certified Organic)

2 cups miniature marshmallows

1. Spray a $1^1/_2$-quart casserole with cooking spray.

2. Put the potatoes, cinnamon and ginger in an electric mixer bowl. Beat at medium speed until almost smooth. Add the broth and beat until potatoes are fluffy. Spoon the potato mixture in the prepared dish. Top with the marshmallows.

3. Bake at 350°F. for 20 minutes or until heated through and marshmallows are golden brown.

Simmered Vegetables

Makes 4 servings

Prep Time: 5 minutes

Cook Time: 15 minutes

1 can (10½ ounces) Campbell's® Condensed Chicken Broth

½ cup water

4 cups cut-up fresh *or* 1 bag (20 ounces) frozen vegetable combination (broccoli, cauliflower, carrots)

Heat the broth, water and vegetables in a 2-quart saucepan over medium-high heat to a boil. Reduce the heat to low. Cover and cook for 5 minutes or until the vegetables are tender. Drain.

Shopping List

Chicken Broth

frozen vegetable combination

Cheddar Broccoli Bake

Makes 6 servings

1 can (10 ³/₄ ounces) Campbell's® Condensed
   Cheddar Cheese Soup

½ cup milk

   Dash ground black pepper

4 cups cooked broccoli cuts

1 can (2.8 ounces) French fried onions (1⅓ cups)

Prep Time: 10 minutes

Bake Time: 30 minutes

1. Stir the soup, milk, black pepper, broccoli and ²/₃ **cup** of the onions in a 1½-quart casserole and cover.

2. Bake at 350°F. for 25 minutes or until hot. Stir the broccoli mixture.

3. Sprinkle the remaining onions over the broccoli mixture. Bake for 5 minutes more or until the onions are golden.

Shopping List

Cheddar Cheese Soup

milk

broccoli

French fried onions

Creamy Corn and Vegetable Orzo

Makes 6 servings

Prep Time: 10 minutes

Cook Time: 10 minutes

Shopping List

butter

green onions

corn

frozen vegetables

orzo

Cream of Celery Soup

2 tablespoons butter

4 medium green onions, sliced (about $1/2$ cup)

2 cups frozen whole kernel corn

1 package (10 ounces) frozen vegetables (chopped broccoli, peas, sliced carrots *or* cut green beans)

$1/2$ of a 16-ounce package rice-shaped pasta (orzo), cooked and drained

1 can ($10\,3/4$ ounces) Campbell's® Condensed Cream of Celery Soup (Regular *or* 98% Fat Free)

$1/2$ cup water

1. Heat the butter in a 12-inch skillet over medium heat. Add the green onions and cook until tender. Add the corn, vegetables and pasta. Cook and stir for 3 minutes.

2. Stir the soup and water into the skillet. Cook and stir for 5 minutes or until mixture is hot and bubbling. Serve immediately.

Savory Vegetables

Makes 4 servings

Prep Time: 5 minutes

Cook Time: 10 minutes

Shopping List

Chicken Broth

vegetables

1 cup Swanson® Chicken Broth (Regular, Natural Goodness® *or* Certified Organic)

3 cups cut-up vegetables (Use a combination of vegetables you like, including broccoli flowerets, cauliflower flowerets, sliced carrots, bell pepper strips, onion wedges *and* snow peas)

1. Heat the broth and vegetables in a 3-quart saucepan over medium-high heat to a boil.

2. Reduce the heat to low. Cover and cook for 5 minutes or until the vegetables are tender-crisp. Drain the vegetables.

Eggs & Breakfast Foods

Fish & Shellfish

VOLUME MEASUREMENTS (dry)

$1/8$ teaspoon = 0.5 mL
$1/4$ teaspoon = 1 mL
$1/2$ teaspoon = 2 mL
$3/4$ teaspoon = 4 mL
1 teaspoon = 5 mL
1 tablespoon = 15 mL
2 tablespoons = 30 mL
$1/4$ cup = 60 mL
$1/3$ cup = 75 mL
$1/2$ cup = 125 mL
$2/3$ cup = 150 mL
$3/4$ cup = 175 mL
1 cup = 250 mL
2 cups = 1 pint = 500 mL
3 cups = 750 mL
4 cups = 1 quart = 1 L

VOLUME MEASUREMENTS (fluid)

1 fluid ounce (2 tablespoons) = 30 mL
4 fluid ounces ($1/2$ cup) = 125 mL
8 fluid ounces (1 cup) = 250 mL
12 fluid ounces ($1 1/2$ cups) = 375 mL
16 fluid ounces (2 cups) = 500 mL

WEIGHTS (mass)

$1/2$ ounce = 15 g
1 ounce = 30 g
3 ounces = 90 g
4 ounces = 120 g
8 ounces = 225 g
10 ounces = 285 g
12 ounces = 360 g
16 ounces = 1 pound = 450 g

DIMENSIONS

$1/16$ inch = 2 mm
$1/8$ inch = 3 mm
$1/4$ inch = 6 mm
$1/2$ inch = 1.5 cm
$3/4$ inch = 2 cm
1 inch = 2.5 cm

OVEN TEMPERATURES

250°F = 120°C
275°F = 140°C
300°F = 150°C
325°F = 160°C
350°F = 180°C
375°F = 190°C
400°F = 200°C
425°F = 220°C
450°F = 230°C

BAKING PAN AND DISH EQUIVALENTS

Utensil	Size in Inches	Size in Centimeters	Volume	Metric Volume
Baking or Cake Pan (square or rectangular)	8×8×2	20×20×5	8 cups	2 L
	9×9×2	23×23×5	10 cups	2.5 L
	13×9×2	33×23×5	12 cups	3 L
Loaf Pan	8½×4½×2½	21×11×6	6 cups	1.5 L
	9×9×3	23×13×7	8 cups	2 L
Round Layer Cake Pan	8×1½	20×4	4 cups	1 L
	9×1½	23×4	5 cups	1.25 L
Pie Plate	8×1½	20×4	4 cups	1 L
	9×1½	23×4	5 cups	1.25 L
Baking Dish or Casserole			1 quart/4 cups	1 L
			1½ quart/6 cups	1.5 L
			2 quart/8 cups	2 L
			3 quart/12 cups	3 L